THE CHILDHOOD OF DREAM'S

THE CHILDHOOD OF DREAM'S

Mohd. Asalam Khan

Translator
Prabhakar Bhatt

YATRA BOOKS
An imprint of Vani Prakashan Group

vaniprakashan.com

First Edition : 2024

YATRA BOOKS
VANI PRAKASHAN GROUP

Head Office

4695, 21-A, Daryaganj, New Delhi-110 002, India
Phone : +91 11 23273167, 11 23275710

Registered Bookstores and Offices

Ashok Rajpath, Patna-800 004, Bihar
Coffee House Campus, Mahatma Gandhi Marg, Allahabad-211 001, Uttar Pradesh
Mahatma Gandhi International Hindi University, Wardha-442 001, Maharashtra
36-A, Shakespeare Sarani, Near Rani Birla Girls College, Kolkata-700017, West Bengal

sales@vaniprakashan.in
vaniprakashan@gmail.com

The Childhood Of Dream's
by Mohd. Asalam Khan
Translated by Prabhakar Bhatt

ISBN : 978-93-5775-783-6
Play

Price : ₹ 490

Printed and bound in India at City Press, Delhi-110 095

Vani Prakashan's signature motif is created by Artist Maqbool Fida Husain

Contents

CHAPTER - 1

Alexander the Great

SCENE - 1

(A view of King Puru's palace, where a royal messenger of Alexander's invading army is waiting for a meeting with the King)

Puru's soldier : Victory to the King. The royal messenger of Alexander the Great wants to see Your Majesty.

Puru : Bring him in.

Messenger : Salutations to Emperor Puru from our Emperor. *(One hand raised in Roman style)*

Puru : Your Emperor has conquered and looted many countries in the past few years. Before reaching Jhelum in Punjab, he has killed thousands of men, women and children. Their blood is flowing in our sacred rivers. What does he want from us now?

Messenger : Alexander the Great desires that, like King Ambhi, you should surrender before his army.

Puru : We will defeat and destroy the army of Alexander.

(Enraged, the messenger's right hand reaches the handle of the sword)

Messenger : By Jupiter, Alexander is out to conquer the world! Remember, when the blood of your army will flow into the waters of Jhelum and Chenab, you will have to answer to your people.

Puru : In the darkness of the night, your army has crossed Jhelum. Hear you, Messenger! We are no fools. You are Alexander the Great, himself disguised as the messenger. If I put you to death for your foolishness, I will not be committing any crime, I am sure.

(There is huge confusion in the court. Alexander smiles. Puru sends for his son, commanding him to prepare for war)

Alexander : I know you cannot be so childish. What face will you show to the world after killing a royal messenger?

Puru : If I like I can get you cut into pieces and feed them to crows and vultures. But no, not here. We will do it in the battlefield

(After a fierce battle, Emperor Puru is brought as prisoner before Alexander)

Alexander : Our army has defeated your forces. We have occupied your entire kingdom.

Puru : Emperor Alexander, you have deceived us. You have attacked my army even after ceasefire. I ask you again: What have you gained by killing millions of young men? You have left mothers crying for their dead sons. Tell me, have you ever been able to sleep peacefully since you and your armies have been murdering people just to expand your empire?

Alexander : Come, come! Say, how shall I treat you?

Puru : Treat me? Treat me the way a king treats another king!

Alexander : Puru, I am very pleased with your answer. I make you, my friend, not my prisoner. In the Greek language, you will be known as Porus. I am also returning your conquered kingdom to you. You have opened my eyes. Alexander and his armies will return to Greece, from here itself. One thing more, here is to our friendship. Alexander has not saluted anyone ever before. *(Stands up with both feet joined and right hand rose in salute)*. Long live Alexander and Porus! Long live Nicator!

CHAPTER - 2

Akbar

Royal door-keeper : Emperor of India, Akbar the Great, is on his way to Deewan-e-Aam, the court of the people.

(There is a huge crowd waiting to catch a glimpse of Akbar. Meanwhile, the emperor arrives).

Soldier : Sir, just to see you my Lord, crowds of Hindus, Muslims and Christians are all lined up, waiting for their turn.

Akbar : Fellow countrymen, let it be known to all that I was born in the fortress of Rana Virsal of Amarkot. Today, I am sitting on the thrown of the Emperor. Born in India, I am an Indian to the core. My grandfather was Babur, father Humayun and mother was Hamida Banu Begum.

Birbal : His Majesty is the third in the line of the great Taimur dynasty.

Akbar : Now I would like to hear my people about their problems. In fact, I would like to know everything about my subjects in whichever part of the country they may be under my rule.

Person 1 : We are from Awadh, Sir. We are traders by occupation. Timber is my trade. It is

Your Majesty's kindness that you are encouraging me to speak out frankly before you. O King, do you know that all Muslim kings before the great Mughals used to take Jiziya tax from us just for being Hindus?

Maan Singh : *(On a signal from Akbar)* Yes, Zill-e-Ilahi (ruler of the world), Qutubuddin Aibak was the first king to impose Jiziya in India.

Akbar : I am very sorry, but there is no such law anywhere else in the world. I abolish it now. Raja Maan Singh, issue an order today itself with the royal seal on it. Well, Raja Todarmal, please explain why was that soldier counting money while we were taking rest in Mathura. We were on our way from Delhi to Agra.

Raja Todarmal : Sir, I had known about it already, but for Your Majesty, it was a new thing.

Akbar : Please begin from the beginning, Raja Todarmal.

Raja Todarmal : There is an old royal order that a Hindu will have to pay the pilgrim tax if he visits a holy place.

(Akbar is furious)

Akbar : I say why did you pay the tax at all? Anyway, here is another royal order. No such taxes will be levied on the people, now onwards.

Abul Fazal : Now, the history of India is beginning to change. Your Majesty, please issue one more order as well. Those who are in jail should not be forced to convert to Islam.

Akbar : Sure, of course. This too must end. You know, I have great regard for my Hindu subjects.

Maan Singh : Your Majesty, the world will always remember the Emperor of India as Akbar the Great for abolishing Jiziya, the pilgrim tax, and forced conversion of prisoners to Islam.

(Akbar Zindabad — Long live Akbar)

Person 2 : May His Majesty stay happy and healthy, forever and ever.

Father Pinto (Christian Missionary): We are petitioners, My Lord. The missionaries wish to pay homage to Akbar the Great. Sir, we are pleased to see you.

(Christians are dressed in priestly clothes).

Akbar : How much hardship, you must have faced during your journey?

Father Pinto : Yes, we did. But what a marvelous policy to govern the people you have chosen, My Lord—peace treaties with smaller kings instead of fights in the battlefields! Today, our British currency is lower than your currency. Your GDP is superior to ours by 25%.

Akbar : Thanks, but tell the purpose of your visit.

Father Pinto : Lord, we are Christian missionaries. We are propagating our faith. We build schools for modern education and hospitals for better health and medical care of the people.

Abul Fazal : We know your purpose. It is to spread your religion.

Father Pinto : But, we shall build hospitals, schools and colleges for education and if the kind emperor permits, we shall build churches also for prayer.

Akbar : Abul Fazal, so now you know, what they are saying. In education and schooling, we are far behind. Perhaps we stand to gain with the arrival of these Christians. I accord my permission to the building of schools, hospitals and churches from Agra to Delhi and to Lahore.

(The darbar is dismissed)

CHAPTER - 3

Raja Ram Mohan Roy

SCENE -1

Keshav : Ram Mohan, you are like an open book, but tell us what made you stand up against the practice of Sati?

Ram Mohan Roy : Keshav, I was about 14, when my elder brother passed away. I saw my sister-in-law being decorated like a bride by other women. On enquiry, my sister-in-law started crying bitterly. She said that my father, her father-in-law, was forcing her to sit on the funeral pyre along with her dead husband. When I talked to my father, he shouted at me, saying "get lost". It pained me greatly. The very thought of a living person being burnt alive brought shivers all over the body. How bitterly would my sister-in-law cry, I was picturing in my imagination.

Keshav : Oh God, horrible! Did she cry?

Roy : Perhaps I was destined to see this ghastly drama to its end. I could not hear the cries of pain of my sister-in-law because of the terrible noise of the beating drums and cymbals.

Keshav : So, this is why you have left your village

Hooghly and your family for Calcutta.

(Enters Devendranath)

Devendranath : Today, not only Calcutta but the whole of Brahmo Samaj of Bengal is criticising idol-worship. It is an empty ritual in the name of the Vedas and the Upanishads.

Keshav : Not only this, polygamy, child marriage and Sati —all these are against the Vedas.

Devendranath : Ram Mohan, let me tell you, the majority in the society is on your side. By the way, what about your plan to visit Delhi and London?

Keshav : Akbar the Second. Poor fellow! He has absolutely no rights of his own.

Ram Mohan : Well, exactly ten days from now, I have to be in the Delhi court. Here is the invitation, already.

Devendranath : Look, Ram Mohan, can Akbar II not issue a royal order against the Sati system?

Keshav : I had read somewhere that this inhuman and cruel subject of Sati had once been raised in the court of Akbar the Great also. But then, Rajput kings were also among the nine jewels – Navratnas of Akbar. Even though Akbar was personally against Sati, it could not be banned.

Ram Mohan : Any way, two centuries have already passed. What matters is that Akbar the Second is quite fond of the books I have written and also supports Brahmo Samaj. He is very kind to me and I must visit him in Delhi on his invitation.

SCENE - 2

(Ram Mohan has a garland of flowers around his neck. Keshav and Devendranath embrace him.)

Devendranath : Looks like that this Delhi story will continue for the whole day.

Ram Mohan : Whatever, but the condition of Akbar the Second is really bad. Much worse than what is being heard. He neither has the throne, nor does the government belong to him. He is actually a puppet of the British.

Keshav : But, did you take up the issue of Sati with him?

Ram Mohan : Yes, I did. After a good deal of thought, Akbar said two things: "Ram Mohan, your ideology and the books you have written have given women many of their rights. For this, I decorate you with the title of Raja." He also encouraged me to go to London to put my case against Sati in the Privy Council. In fact, here is the return fare for journey by ship to London that he has given, but he asked me to do a little job for him also. He said, "Please tell the Privy Council to increase the allowance of your national head."

Devendranath : So, what are you thinking for the future? Any plans?

Ram Mohan : Yes, see, the fare I have received from the Delhi emperor will serve all three of us if we add some more money to it. We can reach London easily. To the question as to how shall we return, I say, leave it in the hands of God, who lives above the sky (smiles at his joke).

SCENE - 3

Keshav : We thought that it was our welcome party. In reality, they are our opponents.

An Englishman : Why has this Hindu Brahmin come to my London? He writes against the Christians in his newspaper.

(Outside, loud slogan-shouting is going on)

Devendranath : We are the subjects of the same sovereign? How can they stop us from getting off the ship?

(After alighting, all three of them made their stay at the home of their women friend, who was the wife of a high ranking English official in Calcutta. Not only that the friend took care of their boarding and lodging but she also made proper advance arrangements with the Privy Council for the date and time of their interview. Ram Mohan Roy remained ever grateful to her friend, Annie Simon. He presented his petition in the Privy Council in 1829).

Ram Mohan : My Lord, I had submitted my petition or request, well in time for your kind consideration in favour of my prayer against the practice of Sati. I would like to know how can there be two sets of laws, one favouring men and the other against women under the same government? I have every hope that one of you is going to be the Governor-General of India very soon and that you will be kind and surely end this grave injustice of the law against women.

Lord William Bentinck : Ram Mohan, I have read your books on Brahmo Samaj and other literature. You know English very well and yet you do not speak it. Why?

Ram Mohan : Sir, actually I know eight languages but Hindi is my mother tongue.

Lord William Bentinck : Okay. All debate and discussion ends here. The Privy Council is in full agreement with Ram Mohan's view. As a result, effective from today, 4 December 1829, the Sati custom is hereby abolished from the British Empire. Those forcing this practice on others will be punished severely.

(Eighteen of Acts passed during the lifetime of Ram Mohan Roy have found a place in the Constitution of India)

(After a long illness, this great social reformer and India's representative in Britain, Raja Ram Mohan Roy, passed away at the home of Annie Simon. Progressive English people were so deeply impressed with him that a statue of Ram Mohan Roy still stands in the centre of a four-road crossing in Bristol.)

CHAPTER - 4

Jallianwala Bagh

April 13, 1919

SCENE 1

(Early morning. A group of persons enter Jallianwala Bagh, close to Amritsar. They are talking among themselves)

Sulkhan : Hey, Suchcha! Listen brother, it is something very important. We are meeting here to show our anger against the Rowlatt Act and we are also celebrating our own Baisakhi Festival.

Suchcha : Today is April 13 but this black law was passed some two months back by the Parliament in London in February 1919.

Udham Singh : I say, do you know the purpose of this law? The purpose is to arrest our freedom fighters without warrant and without permission from the courts.

Sulkhan : Mahatma Gandhi has strongly condemned this law. He has even called the English devils.

Suchcha : So, let us not forget that Gandhiji already has made his stand clear. Only a week ago, he had said that we will follow the divine path of non-violence and civil disobedience. In my opinion, this old mahatma will surely win and get the better of the British Government and make them yield.

Sulkhan : See, the people have already started coming. Let us get ready for peaceful march and our "prabhatpheri". *(Informers of the British police have passed on the news of the "prabhatpheri" to higher authorities)*

Suchcha : Not very far from the Golden Temple, we have always celebrated Baisakhi in Jallianwala Bagh surrounded by its 15-foot high brick wall. On behalf of the Congress Committee and my own behalf, I greet you all, my dear friends – Happy Baisakhi to everybody.

Sulkhan : Baisakhi, of course, yes, but our main objective is to oppose the Rowlatt Act. This means they can arrest our freedom fighters without warrant and without court trial. They will enter our houses and torture us. This meeting supports the call of our national leaders that the Rowlatt Act must end.

(The English General Dyer enters Jallianwala Bagh with his troops and orders them to open fire without warning to shoot unarmed innocent men, women and children. Old and young -- all of them. There are screams and loud shoutings. People run around, this way and that way. To save their lives, many jump into a nearby well. In the pile of dead, Udham Singh escapes death.)

SCENE-2

(1940 Caxton Hall, Westminster, London)

(The function is heading to its end. Retired General Dyer is about to start his presidential speech when two shots are fired in the air. There is total confusion and chaos. Guests run around, screaming in panic.)

Udham Singh : You all can leave the auditorium peacefully. I will not harm any of you except that I need the dictator and retired General Dyer.

(In the wink of an eye, a bullet strikes Dyer's left shoulder. The hall empties. Only Dyer and Udham Singh remain on the stage)

General Dyer : Who are you? What wrong have I done to you? What is this long-nursed enmity? I know nothing about it!

Udham Sing : So, you know nothing? If I like I can empty this revolver of the remaining three bullets. But, no, I must answer your questions and also ask you questions of my own.

General Dyer : I say again, what for? Why this punishment? You do not realise, man, the police will be here any moment. They will catch hold of you and will send you to the gallows.

Udham Singh : In that hell-hole of the Andaman Jail – we call it Kalapani; you hung to death three of our patriots every day. But this has failed to terrorise us. Who cares for your two-inch gallows?

General Dyer : But, our government has closed down the Andaman Cellular Jail.

Udham Singh : So what? My first question to you Dyer is: Did you open fire on a non-violent demonstration of children, women, young men and old men? Very young children, sobbing babies, you killed them all.

Dyer : Yes, absolutely right.

Udham Singh : My second question now. You had brought cannon to Jallianwala Bagh, close to Amritsar. And because the lane leading to the entrance to the Bagh was narrow, so narrow that the cannon could not pass through it, so you left it there. If it were possible to take the cannon inside, you would have made mince meat of hundreds of innocent human beings. Is it not?

Dyer : You are right, again. I had ordered the cannon for this purpose only.

Udham Singh : So…… So….. when the cannon failed to fit into your evil design, you riddled the bodies of countless hundreds with deadly shots. Bad luck for you, Devil. A badly wounded young man still managed to come out alive from the heap of the dead and dying. And that young man swore by his motherland – Bharat Mata -- that he would not be a true Sikh, until he had killed that Demon, that you are, Dyer, and I am that young man, who refused to die. Here you are, now.

(Fires all three remaining shots)

(After a court trial, Udham Singh was hanged to death on July 31, 1940)

CHAPTER - 5

'Simon Commission Go Back'

SCENE -1

(Four Congress members sitting on chairs)

Yusuf J. Meherally : This secret meeting of today is taking place at Dongri Sarai. It is a locality in Bombay city. Now, I invite Mr Mohammad Ali Jinnah to the mike. He is a frontline leader of the party. Mr Jinnah, please.

Mr Jinnah : Friends, it happened only last week. I had gone to Pune from Calcutta to attend a party meeting. There I met Gandhiji. When I asked him about the Simon Commission, he explained things very easily. He said that there were two main issues. First, the English are looking for support from sympathetic political parties to frame a new Constitution for the country, anyhow. Second, why are they so hell-bent upon it that all members of the Commission are only English and not a single one of them is Indian? I, therefore, suggest: Spread out, follow the Commission wherever it goes and oppose it stoutly. Non-violently, of course!

(Jinnah resumes his seat)

Meherally : Now, opposition is the word. I learnt last night that the British ship will soon be anchored at the Bombay sea port. Our slogan will be: "Simmon Commission Go Back".

(On 3 February 1928, Maharashtra Congress workers and the citizens of Bombay staged historic public strike on the call of Jinnah. Everything came to a grinding halt and nothing moved. Not even tea stalls or pan shops were open. From morning till midnight, Meherally's call of "Simon Commission Go Back" echoed and reverberated throughout the mega city of Bombay. After that it became the litany of nation -- Simon Commission Go Back. It followed the Commission all over the country, to whichever city it went.)

SCENE 2

(Mr Simon and his six members are staying in the army guest house in Lahore on 29 October 1928. A view of the road opposite the guest house, where Lala Lajpat Rai, a leader of the so-called Garam Dal (an extremist faction) of the Congress is standing, surrounded by a huge crowd. The public meeting starts on its own.)

Lajpat Rai : You have power. You have the army. You have weapons. We are followers of non-violent Gandhiji. Our peaceful Congress Committee has three questions to ask of you. Answer please.

Number 1 : When did we say to you that we want a Commission?

Number 2 : Your Commission is all English, all seven of you. Why is there not a single Indian member in it?

And Number 3 : The entire nation knows that you want to make a very soft and pliable Constitution to strangle us, so that we will not be able to even breathe.

{(Addressing the crowd) I call on you all to shout "Simon Commission Go Back"}.

(The British Indian Police lathicharge the crowd, raining cruel blows on the people. In the melee, Lala Lajpat Rai gets badly wounded. In spite of treatment, he dies on November 17, 1928).

CHAPTER 6

Bhagat Singh

Born: September 27, 1907

Died: March 23, 1931, Lahore Jail

SCENE OF ACTION: LAHORE

(Two young revolutionaries, Rajguru and Sukhdev, are sitting in a room)

Rajguru : Hope, all is well. It is so late. Why has Bhagat Singh not returned yet? I wonder whether he has eaten food at all.

Sukhdev : Hey Guru listen, our Lalaji was hit by lathis on 13th October. Today is the 17. Leave improvement alone, he is getting bad to worse. I am worried about him.

(Bhagat Singh enters the room. He is weeping and is inconsolable. His friends rush and hold him softly in arms).

Bhagat Singh : Oh, my….. Hey Sukhdev, Lalaji is gone. Now he is a martyr.

(All three clasp together and cry bitterly)

Wipe these tears. Tears weaken freedom fighters. We will have to take revenge of the death of Lalaji.

Rajguru : This police officer, John Saunders, comes out of his office at 11 in the morning.

Sukhdev : There is a "lassi stall" nearby.

Bhagat Singh : That is fine. We will kill the wretched fellow, there itself.

Rajguru : Now, the earth will tremble under the feat of the British. It will be a good lesson for the killers.

Bhagat Singh : It will be like sounding a new bugle of revolution all over the country. We must reach the gurudwara at 7 sharp in the morning. With the revolver. From there, we will move on to the lassi stall.

SCENE - 2

(Early in the morning. Sukhdev and Bhagat Singh, both with revolvers, are close to the stall. John Saunders comes out of the police office. As he approaches the centre of the stage, he is encircled by three revolutionaries and in the blink of an eye; Bhagat Singh makes him the target of his revolver. Meanwhile, on hearing shots being fired, some policemen rush in)

Rajguru : You are Indians. There is no fight between us. We have to kill this John Saunders. And he is lying here dead on the ground before us.

Sukhdev : O! Let us go now before a full battalion comes marching.

(Next morning. The newspaper hawker is on the stage)

Hawker : Murder of John Saunders – the killer of Lalaji. Revolutionaries have shot him.

SCENE - 3

(Bhagat Singh reaches Delhi in disguise. In Delhi, he needs his new colleague, Batukeshwar Dutt.)

Batukeshwar : Bhagat, so how did it go? I hope there was Nnothing to bother about during the journey?

Bhagat Singh : *(Laughs)* What to bother about? Name, address and face, all are changed. Brand new everything, no question of getting bothered.

Batukeshwar : Here, in the Central Legislative Assembly, Delhi, two bills are being debated – the Public Safety Bill and the Trade Disputes Bill. Of course, it is for the interest of the British Government. If the bills are passed, the country will suffer greatly.

Bhagat Singh : We will not let it happen. But, I am a stranger here and I don't know my way around.

Batukeshwar : You just stay close to me. Together, we will make it to the public gallery of the Assembly.

(Batukeshwar Dutt hands over a bomb to Bhagat Singh which he keeps in the pockets of his overcoat. The next movement, as they reach the public gallery, there are two loud blasts, one after the other. Both of them shout "Inquilab Zindabad" and and shower leaflets. People start running here and there to save their lives. Actually, it was just the cracker bombs, not actual

bombs. It made a lot of noise but did not hurt anyone. None was injured.)

Batukeshwar : Please, please do not panic! We mean no harm to anyone. We are simply protesting against the Trade Bill, which this government is trying to pass in the Assembly.

Bhagat Singh : This bill protects the owners and not the workers. It is for the government but against the government servants. The bill serves the interests of the dictator and capitalists. We will never allow it to be passed.

Batukeshwar : Bhagat, we have enough time and I know the way to escape from here.

Bhagat Singh : We have not come here to throw the bomb and run away. We have come here to awaken the country. So, this is how it is. Do not be afraid. Let them arrest us and present before the court.

(In no time, the police arrest both of them. Later, Bhagat Singh, Sukhdev and Rajguru were hanged to death on March 23, 1931 in Lahore Jail, while Batukeshwar Dutt was sentenced to life imprisonment.)

CHAPTER 7

Gandhiji's Railway Journey (South Africa)

7 June 1893

Presenter : After obtaining a law degree from London, Gandhiji could not find enough legal work for himself in the courts of Rajkot and Bombay. Meanwhile, he was offered appointment by an Indian businessman, Abdullah, in South Africa to work in his company. Thus, Gandhiji found himself in Durban *(South Africa)* where he caught a train for Pretoria. Five minutes were to go before the train would leave. Gandhiji entered a first class bogey with his luggage where his seat was already reserved. He was holding a book in his hand by John Ruskin, a very famous English writer of his times. As the train moved, Gandhiji opened the book and was soon lost in reading it. It was past 11 o'clock in the night, when a railway ticket examiner – TTE -- entered the Gandhiji's bogey. Gandhiji was dressed in a suit.

TTE : Where are you going?

Gandhiji : Pretoria.

TTE : Show me your ticket.

Gandhiji : *(Promptly takes out the ticket from his pocket to show)* Here is my ticket.

TTE : How did you get the ticket?

Gandhiji : I got it through wire.

TTE : Well, you will have to get down with your luggage at the next station, Pietermaritzburg.

Gandhiji : Look here, I have a law degree from a London college. *(Shows his visiting card)* I have been appointed to plead a case in a South African court.

TTE : You black man, you are all like coolies. If you do not remove yourself and your luggage at the next station, I will throw you out along with your luggage.

(Enters a Negro coolie)

Coolie : Look like, Sir, you are a new arrival. This is how the law works here.

(After sometime the train reaches Pietermaritzbur station. Gandhiji does not alight from the train. The railway guard is also there. They catch hold of Gandhiji and push him out of the bogey -- his two bags meeting the same fate. Gandhiji falls flat on his face and is deeply hurt. The train whistles on. Gandhiji nurses his wounds on the face and the head, as well as his humiliation. He sits down on a bench nearby and begins talking to himself -- entering a soliloquy.)

Gandhiji : My God! I have never thought that a

human being can humiliate another human being with such cruelty. I feel like going back to India, right now, from here itself. But to return like this will be sheer cowardice. God, give me strength to answer this colour distinction -- apartheid -- and put an end to such in human persecution by the British Government, once and for all.

(Gandhiji is suddenly enveloped in an orb of light)

Soul of Gandhiji : What a lonely night! What a strange country! What is troubling you?

Gandhiji : But, who are you? Why can't I see you?

Soul : Do not waste your time on these idle questions, Mohandas.

Gandhiji : Oh, I see. You seem to know everything about me, that I have been bundled out of the train because of my colour. I have already decided to put up a fight against this colour bar. This is an inhuman policy of the government. Fight I will, but with what weapon to fight, I do not know.

Soul : Karamchand, I am as badly hurt as you are. This is why I am here, by your side. I will tell you about a weapon, which can overthrow this government from its seat.

Gandhiji : What is that weapon? May I know?

Soul : "Ahimsa Parmo Dharma" *(Non-violence is the ultimate religion)*. As to the rest, you seem to be an intelligent person. I have shown you the way. Now, it is for you to follow it to your destination.

CHAPTER - 8

Champaran

(On the stage – the frontage of the Zamindar's (landlord) mansion where the Zamindar and the police officer are talking together)

Zamindar : Sir, you know very well. What great shirkers are our farmers!

Mr Richard : Why? Anything special?

Zamindar : Yes Sir. This time, the production of Indigo (Neel) in Champaran has been less.

Mr Richard : Well, Zamindar, you know very well that the British are fighting in the First World War and so we need more production and money.

Zamindar : The 3/20 tinkathia law is not making the soil fertile. On the other hand, the soil is turning barren every day. In fact, you may see it yourself, if you like, Sir.

Mr Richard : Did you not tell the farmers that if they do not sow 3/20 kathia neel, they will go to jail?

Zamindar : Richard Sahib, you better see things for yourself.

(Both of them come to the expose part of the stage)

Mr Richard : *(To the farmers working in the field)* Why are you not growing Indigo crop, I mean Neel?

(Mr Richard starts beating a farmer so savagely with his cane that he falls down to the ground)

Mr Zamindar, arrest the bastard.

(Enters Gandhiji on the stage and listens to the painful story of the former)

Farmer : For many years, the English have been forcing us to cultivate the Indigo as a crop. But the 3/20 kathia Neel law has been enforced from April 10, 1917 only. It means we will have to sow Indigo in our fields at the cost of going to jail because this is what the kathia law says.

(A meeting is held on the stage)

Gandhiji : This is the government policy that farmers of Champaran must grow Kathia Neel in their fields under the 3/20 law, then I call upon them, all of them, that no farmer will sow Neel as a crop. If they do so, they will be beaten, persecuted or jailed. So now the scenario is that no farmer will grow Indigo in their fields under any condition.

Kripalani : It is the wish of Gandhiji that we should all proceed to file a written complaint with Lt. Governor Sir Andrew Gett for the solution of our problem.

(Slogans of Long Live Mahatma Gandhi – Mahatma Gandhi Ki Jai)

Gandhiji : Lt. Governor Sir Andrew Gett has written a letter to me saying that the old Indigo law of 3/20 is being abolished with immediate effect from 3rd October 1917.

Kripalani : This was Gandhiji's first Non-Cooperation and Civil Disobedience movement and it was successful.

Farmer : Gandhiji, you are our saviour. God has sent you, you are our Mahatma.

(This was the first time that Gandhiji was called "Mahatma")

CHAPTER - 9

Chauri-Chaura incident

February 4, 1922

SCENE - 1

(Inspector Gupteshwar Singh and Sub Inspector Prithvi Pal are talking together)

Prithvi Pal : Inspector Sahib, don't worry. Bashir will just be here.

Gupteshwar : These Congress workers seem to have gone off their head. I had told Hukum Singh to apply to the chowki (Police Post) for permission to send reinforcement. But then, be gentle and no one listens to you.

(Enters constable Bashir Khan)

Bashir Khan : Sahib, the meeting has started. There are around 3,000 to 4,000 people.

Gupteshwar : But you had said that Maulana is known to you and he would persuade and manage everything.

Bashir Khan : Maulana Sahib said that after the Jallianwala episode, things have gone out of his hands. Now whether your police beat us with lathis or throw us behind the bars, we are prepared for both.

Prithvi Pal : Now see, Sir, how things are. These

Congress people care two hoots for the law.

Gupteshwar : All right then. It is time to teach them a lesson. Ask the soldiers to proceed to the action spot and, yes, tell them to load their rifles.

SCENE - 2

Scene of Action

Prithvi Pal : Hukum Singh Ji, you know Section 144 has been declared in Chauri Chaura since yesterday. This meeting is against the law.

(Hukum Singh on the stage)

Hukum Singh : I know nothing about Section 144, and in this small town what is the need for police permission to hold a meeting? So, friends *(addresses the crowd)*, as I was saying, this is a condolence meeting for that recent Jallianwala Bagh tragedy.

Gupteshwar : Once again I am telling you all that: This meeting is illegal and it is against the British Government.

(Three soldiers get down to the ground on one knee and take aim with their rifles at the target. With Gupteshwar ordering "Fire", the guns roar and hit Hukum Singh, Maulana Sarwar and another person in the heart. Some young men stare in the eyes of the policemen and rush at them. The constables run away in fear. The crowd is in hot pursuit behind them. To save their lives, the policemen take shelter in the chowki. The angry crowd gathers around the chowki and set it on fire. In the arson, 22 policemen are burnt to death.

SCENE - 3

February 12, 1922

(In a room at Sabarmati Ashram, Gandhiji, Patel and Nehru are talking about Chauri Chaura incident among themselves)

Nehru : Bapu, this newspaper article has given a very detailed description of the entire Chauri Chaura business.

Patel : Three Congress workers and 22 policemen have died. It is sad, very sad news really. The English have given it an international colour.

Nehru : Bapu, we are trying our best that the accused must be punished. The police have already arrested some 14 suspects.

Gandhiji : I had received all the information on the 4th February itself. Those who have been arrested and sent to jail will not return. I had never thought even in my dreams that the non-violence movement of mine will end up like this.

Patel : Perhaps, those who were opposed to your idea of non-violence at the Calcutta conference had planned it in advance.

Nehru : Patel Sahib, there were also other causes of opposition.

Gandhiji : Actually, the full meaning of the

Non-cooperation Movement or Civil Disobedience is not known to the people. Non-violence is just non-violence. There is no place at all for violence in it. Nehruji, you are very young. There is no English conspiracy that the whole world knows about the Chauri Chaura. This has been possible because of the fearless international media.

Nehru : Gandhiji, I think, it is like killing two birds with one stone.

Gandhiji : You are right. The first stone has struck the Non-cooperation Movement and the second has hit Mohandas *(Gandhi)*.

Patel : Do not be so upset, Bapu. In our own country, you know, besides Naram Dal *(moderate section)* even Garam Dal *(extremist section)* is emerging.

Gandhiji : Here is the letter. Jawaharji, please give it to *The Hindu (newspaper)* so that it is published in the next morning edition.

Nehru : *(Reads the letter)* Bapu, please don't do it. It will hurt the people. *(Nehru hands over the letter to Patel)*.

Gandhiji : Look, I had already made up my mind, before you both came here. I announce the withdrawal of Non-cooperation Movement with immediate effect.

Patel : Let us move, Nehruji, the office of *The Hindu* is on the way. This letter must reach there as quickly as possible.

(Patel and Nehru are seen coming out of the Sabarmati Ashram)

CHAPTER - 10

Chandra Shekhar Azad

Birth – July 23, 1906, Death – February 27, 1931

SCENE -1

(On the stage, sits Chandra Shekhar Azad, dressed in dhoti with a secret thread (Janeu) across his bare body, hands clasped behind, rolled pointed mustaches, muscular physique)

Police Officer : Father's name?

Chandra Shekhar : Freedom!

Police Officer : Your name?

Chandra Shekhar : Azad!

Police Officer : Your address?

Chandra Shekhar : Jail!

Police Officer : Soldier, these are the orders of Judge Dharam Dev. Strike him 15 lashes *(One by one, Chandra Shekhar is lashed 15 times).*

Chandra Shekhar : *(At every strike of the lash)* – Vande Matram...Vande Matram..!

(A voice from the crowd)

Voice : Not Chandra Shekhar now, from today, the world will know you as Chandra Shekhar Azad.

SCENE - 2

August 25, 1925, Kakori Train Dacoity

(A morning in Kakori Town. Sounds of shots being fired. Chandra Shekhar Azad and Ram Prasad Bismil appear on the stage with the government money looted from the railway iron box. Azad hits the lock of the box with his foot. The lock breaks open.)

Bismil : Look here, at this money. First, the English looted it from us and now we have looted it from the English. (Smiles)

Chandra Shekhar : This dacoity will enrage the English government, to no end. The world will know it as the "Kakori Kand".

Ashafaqullah Khan: Now, what next?

Bismil : You take this cash to Patna. There, Lala Ram will arrange for new supply of arms. By the way Ashfaq, what is going on in your mind?

Ashfaq : Nothing. But this Kakori dacoity is no ordinary dacoity. This is a new way to awaken the English government from its sleep. This is the revolutionary method.

Lahri : I say, let us disperse by different routes.

Chandra Shekhar : There is one problem. Thakur, Ashfaq and Pandit Ji -- you all are from Shahjahanpur!

Bismil : So what? There is nothing to worry about. All of us will meet at the place appointed by you, 15 days from now. And, Lahri, what is the use... I mean what will you do in Shahjahanpur?

(From one side of the mango grove, sharp sounds of police whistles and firing shots emerge. Countering the firing, all three disappear in thick Dussehri Mango grove.)

SCENE - 3

(February 27, 1931)

(There is a tree and a masonry platform in the centre of the stage)

Chandra Shekhar : Sukhdev, the danger of informers is always everywhere, and so is in Allahabad.

Sukhdev : The British Government does not seem to be yielding. I am thinking to retire to the village with my friend for a few days.

Chandra Shekhar : *(Pulling out a pistol from the fold of his dhoti at the waist)* Not a bad idea at all. You can meet friends and relatives in the village *(hands over the revolver to Sukhdev)*. Keep it friend. It may come handy.

(Outside the Alfred Park, the superintendent of police Sir John Weaver and his deputy Bisheshwar Singh arrive together. Identifying with the description of an informer, Weaver takes a careful aim and shoots Azad. The bullet pierces the thigh clean and goes to the other side.)

Chandra Shekhar : *(Groaning in pain)* Sukhdev, now both of you escape from the other side. Quick.

(In no time, Bisheshwar Singh fires and the bullet hits Azad in the right shoulder)

Pulling himself up with great courage, Azad, a great shooter himself, now targets Bisheshwar Singh and his very first strike smashes the jaw of the DSP. Meanwhile, the police force closes in, surrounding the Jamun tree behind which Azad was hiding himself. He was now left with one single bullet only. He knew that escape was impossible and death was staring him in the face. He decided then that he would not die at the hands of the English, at any cost. He loudly shouts, his favourite slogan: Azad is Azad and will remain Azad.

(He puts the revolver to his temple and shoots the last bullet which shatters his skull. Supreme self-sacrifice at the altar of the motherland by Azad, the warrior patriot.)

CHAPTER - 11

Bharat Ratna Bhimrao Ambedkar

Born: Mhow, Madhya Pradesh, April 14, 1891
Died: Delhi, December 6, 1956

(There are two persons in the centre of the stage talking together)

Sir Daniel : Ambedkar, I have not seen a scholar like you!

Ambedkar : I consider myself to be very fortunate for your cooperation and guidance in research work.

Sir Daniel : There is one thing, which I do not understand.

Ambedkar : What is that, Sir?

Sir Daniel : When you have already acquired a PhD degree in 1915 from Columbia University, what was the need for a second PhD? I think your first subject of research was Commerce in Ancient India?

Ambedkar : You are right, Sir. India is a slave country. Earlier, we paid in silver for our imports but developed countries like the USA, England, France and Germany changed over from silver to gold, devaluing the Indian Rupee. Ever since, we have been in deficit -- call it loss, if you like.

Sir Daniel : So, to find an answer to this question the Rupee, you did the second PhD, tracing the origin of the trouble and finding its solution. You hold, I am told, a double PhD in Economics? I say, what are you up to?

Ambedkar : First of all, I want a Government Bank in my country -- I mean Reserve Bank of India.

Sir Daniel : And, what is the second reason – may I know?

Ambedkar : Sir, we have still plenty of gold in the country but not in the hands of the people of India. Religious places are lush with gold!

Sir Daniel : This gold is of no use to anyone!

Ambedkar : Is not it strange, Sir? Your country is emptying our national treasure and we are stuffing our religious place with gold.

Sir Daniel : Do you know who is profiting the most from it?

Ambedkar : All countries are benefitting from it, Sir, but America, I think, tops the rest. Today, one dollar is equal to three rupees.

Sir Daniel : Well, you are leaving tomorrow, I think? Best of luck then. *(Embraces warmly)*

CHAPTER - 11A

Constituent Assembly

SCENE - 1

(Jogendra Nath Mandal and Ambedkar in discussion)

Ambedkar : Mandal Dada, you are here because of the hard work of our Dalit brothers and support from the Muslim League. I have also been elected to the Constituent Assembly but my own city of Bombay made me lose by 14,374 votes in spite of my two PhDs and dozens of degrees.

Mandal Dada : No doubt about it. You are the most intelligent person in the country, today. But my dear, this is politics. Here, the Congress is the strongest pillar of freedom.

Ambedkar : My objective, to be in the Constituent Assembly, was to be with the leaders of the country.

(The hawker drops the newspaper)

Mandal : Aha, here is the latest news. The *Ananda Bazar Patrika* is here. *(Reading the headlines, he suddenly goes silent)*

Ambedkar : What is the news? I do not know your language.

Mandal : Ambedkar Babu, the news is not good. The Radcliffe Committee Report has shown that your constituency has gone to Pakistan as per Partition.

Ambedkar : So, in a way even after winning my Constituent Assembly seat, I am a loser. Now I had better moved to Delhi today itself. That will do me well.

SCENE - 2

(First sitting of the Constituent Assembly)

N. Gopalaswami Ayyangar : The All India Congress Committee welcomes all the members elected from different provinces to this first sitting of the Constituent Assembly. Now, I request Pandit Nehru to come forward and suggest the name of the Constitution Drafting Committee of the Constituent Assembly.

Nehru : As you all know, the objcctive of the Constituent Assembly is to define the future of India. I mean the future political and administrative structure of free India. Now, who will frame the Constitution? Who will write it? How is it all going to be done? Above all, the question is who will preside over the committee to draft the Constitution? The top leaders of the country have authorised me to take this decision. In exercise of this right, I choose the name of Dr Ambedkar as president of the committee which will draft the Constitution of India. We have at last succeeded in Dr Ambedkar's re-election to the Constituent Assembly from Bombay city.

Ayyangar : I am in full agreement with Nehruji's proposal. I gladly second it. If other members agree with me, they may kindly raise their hands *(all raise hands)*.

Nehru : The first time I met Dr Ambedkar was in the Columbia University. Before you say something, I congratulate you Dr Ambedkar on your election as president of the Constitution Drafting Committee. Let me also add that among your colleagues, there may be some members, possibly against you. The Congress does not believe in caste, creed, untouchability, etc. but firmly believe in the merit of an individual. You have earned 26 scholarly degrees, nationally and internationally. You hold two PhDs in Economics alone. Not only barrister in law, you are also M.Sc. and D.Sc.

Ambedkar : Today, your words have fully healed scratches of my heart, Nehruji. I have closely studied the Constitution of the USA, Soviet Union, Germany and France. I will try my best to live up to your expectations.

(With gesture of thanks, takes a seat)

SCENE - 3

Ayyangar : Dr Ambedkar has worked in a wide social and political sphere. For instance, only recently the English have reduced the working time for their labour from 14 hrs to 8 hrs after publication of a research paper of Dr Ambedkar's *(clapping in the hall).*

(The Indian Constitution was adopted on 26 January 1950. Later, on the question of delaying the Hindu Code Bill, Dr Ambedkar resigned from the cabinet. This bill demanded gender equality in marriage and inheritance. Dr Ambedkar remained a member of the Rajya Sabha until the end of his life. He had accepted Buddhist faith in Nagpur in the presence of about four lakh people.)

CHAPTER 12

Abraham Lincoln

Born: February 12, 1809, Kentucky, USA

Died: April 15, 1865, Peterson house, Washington, DC, USA

(An election meeting of Abraham Lincoln)

Lincoln : Friends, this huge crowd of supporters gives me great joy and hope. I am now convinced of the victory of my Republican Party in the election. You know it already. I am the candidate of this party for the post of the President of the USA.

I have said many things in my election manifesto, but the most important is my promise to abolish slavery from the country, if I am elected President. I will declare slavery illegal and let us not forget that like us, millions of non-whites are also citizens of this country. Their condition is really pitiable. The fifty states that make America, their rights will also be discussed collectively.

Hannibal : Perhaps, you are forgetting Lincoln that the Constitutional Union Party has great influence in the southern state of America. Also, our countrymen have a large number of non-whites working for them in their fields and farm houses. Therefore, many in our own party also want the slavery system to continue, the civil war is quite possible in the country.

(Abraham Lincoln's party won the elections but with a small majority.)

Lincoln : I, my ancestors and my parents, all salute this great nation of America. I am grateful to one and all, whether they have voted for me or not for making me the President of the United States of America. What am I? I am a poor lawyer, born in a labourer's house. I no more belong to any section of the party now. I am the President of the USA. Now, it is the time to think of my most important promise. The promise I made in my manifesto -- I, hereby abolish the practice of slavery…

(People from two opposite sides come to the centre of the stage and begin to exchange blows... representing the civil wars. Vice President Hannibal enters the President's Chamber)

Hannibal : Mr President, the civil war has broken out in the country. The southern states are annoyed with the victory of our party. Carolina, Mississippi, Florida, Alabama, Georgia, Louisiana and Texas have separated from the Union and elected Jefferson David their President.

Lincoln : Mr Vice-President, I have never thrown up my hands even under the most difficult conditions. I say, have a little coffee.

(Vice-President sipping coffee)

This is our instant decision. Give service to the newly-freed slaves in the Army. Strong and sincere working slaves from southern states will cross over to our side. The southern states should be allowed no contact with any foreign country. Whatever be the cost!

Hannibal : Yes Sir, and so it will be. The civil war might subside, on its own perhaps!

(America emerged safe and sound from the trap of slavery. Maybe Lincoln was destined to do bigger deeds. But while he was watching a play, a disgruntled stage actor Wilkes Booth shot him dead on April 14, 1865.)

CHAPTER - 13

Swami Vivekanand

Born: January 12, 1863, Calcutta

Died: July 4, 1902, Belur Math, Howrah

Servant : *(Addressing Paramhans)* Swami Ji, a young boy Narendra Nath Dutt wants to meet you.

Paramhans : Go, bring in the guest.

(Servant escorts Narendra)

Narendra : Pranaam, Paramhans Ji.

Paramhans : Tell me son, what brings you here?

Narendra : I am told religious discussions are held here.

(Paramhans is greatly impressed with Narendra Nath)

Paramhans : Now, that you have come here, on your own, be my chief disciple.

Narendera : I don't understand!

Paramhans : I mean you take to Sanyas *(renunciation)* from today itself. I can see the glow of wisdom inside you.

(Narendra bends and puts his head on the feet of the Paramhans)

Narendra : This is my good luck. I have studied literature, philosophy and history and tried to imbibe Hindu religion and culture.

Paramhans : I ordain you to be a Sanyasi *(monk)* with the name of Vivekanand.

Narendra : I dedicate myself, my entire life to Swami Ramkrishna Paramhans.

(Vivekanand served his master, Swami Ramkrishna Paramhans till the latter's last breath) Thereafter, while propagating spiritual knowledge throughout the country at the age of 25, he reaches Bombay where his admirers and disciples arrange for his voyage to America.

(On May 31, 1893, he left Bombay for Chicago in America. The saffron robe he was wearing was insufficient for the cold of Chicago. With no proper place to stay, Vivekanand had to take shelter for one week in a goods train bogey parked in the railway yard. On September 11, 1893, Swami Vivekanand got the chance to address the Parliament of Religions at the very end of the opening session.)

Vivekanand : My dear brothers and sisters of America *(thunderous clapping in the hall for a few minutes)*, I express my gratitude for your kind and loving welcome. I thank you on behalf of the oldest order of Sanyasis in the world and greet all sects and communities on behalf of millions and millions of Hindus. I take pride in being the follower of a religion which has taught to the world the lesson of tolerance and universal love. We accept all the religions of the world to be true. I feel proud that I am from a country which has welcomed and sheltered countless persons persecuted in other countries in the name of religion. We have nurtured the sacred memories of Jews ousted from their religious places by the Roman invaders after reducing them into ruins. We gave shelter to the Parsis also. Like the many rivers with different origins that fall into the sea in the end, human beings also choose separate routes but in the last they all lead to only God. This Parliament of Religions, I consider it to be a very pious meeting of people. It is a proof of the principles described in the Gita! The communal extremism and its horrible offshoots have kept the world in its stranglehold for a long time. How many times, the earth has been painted red with blood? How many times civilisations have been destroyed? If such things had not happened, humanity would have been far more advanced. Today, the loud message from this meeting of world religions will put an end to all ill-will and bitterness in human minds caused by the sword or the sermon.

If thinking helps in doing good to others, it has value. Otherwise, it is a garbage heap of evil. The sooner we get rid of poisonous thoughts, the better. Thank, you all!

CHAPTER 14

Attack Heart

[One-act Play]

(A boy narrates a story over a mike)

Angry with my wife, I picked up the gun and left Lucknow for Katarniaghat. I stayed with Rukayya until the evening. With darkness approaching, I got out for the hunt. I had been moving on foot for about two hours. The eye which could once spot the big cat from a distance has now weakened. This is why my wife has made me swear against going on a hunt. Mistaking it for a bush, I fell into a 10-foot deep and 20-foot wide ditch, though someone had put thorny branches around the hole as a warning. There were four animals in total in the hole. First, I, the second was a 10-20 foot long python, the third was a horned stag and the fourth, after peering carefully, I found it to be a man-eater. The python opened its mouth and began swallowing the stag. I was watching it. But the lion was watching me, perhaps wondering, how come a real human being-like-thing has come so close to me? The python had, meanwhile, nearly swallowed up the deer but was grappling with its horns. Before dying, it had cast off its slough. My gun was aimed at the lion but I had forgotten to bring cartridges from home. In anger, I put the gun on my shoulder and turned towards the lion. Finding a human being rushing at him, the lion suffered an instant cardiac arrest (heart attack). I attacked the lion with the butt of the gun and with my feet. The lion died because all of his three arteries were choked. No one believes in this Katarniaghat episode even today. But when this humble self returned home, it was with the skin of the python and the skin of the lion, dangling on my right shoulder.

CHAPTER 15

Beware of the Dogs (Humour)

(One-act Play)

It happened during the summers. Our school campus was fenced with wire (but was not barbed). I was playing basketball, when Navin called me. He said he had seen two ripe 'bel' fruits. I said I could accompany him after the game. What game, said Navin, "You are all alone, playing with the girls." I said, "It is a practice match. It will take 10 minutes to end." After the match, both of us, crossing the music room, jumped out of the school campus. On the way, there was a bungalow of one Colonel. On the name plate of the house was written: Beware of the Dogs. His boundary wall was about 4-feet high. The bungalow of the Colonel was in the middle of the boundary. In between the bungalow and boundary wall stood the 'bel' tree. I told Navin, "I can bring down the 'bel' fruit with a stone-throw from here itself." One aimed stone stuck by me and both the 'bel' fruits were down on the ground. Now the question was to pick them from the other side of the wall. Navin was an "expert thief". He was shorter by about 6 inches in height than me. We decided to climb the boundary wall to reach the tree with an alert eye for the Colonel's dogs. We managed to reach the 'bel' fruits but hardly had we bent to pick them when the Colonel released the dogs at us. In the blink of an eye, I threw the fruits across the boundary wall and in one quick leap, I was also out in the open. Navin had also nearly made it, but his one foot was still hanging down the boundary wall when one of the dogs gripped the heel of his foot. Navin screamed. It was very painful for him and he cried bitterly. I picked a piece of wood lying nearby and hit the dog. Navin's foot was badly hurt and wounded. A doctor was needed urgently. A cyclist was passing by but he refused to help saying, "It is a police case." When another cyclist came I rushed to him. I was nervous. Pointing to Navin, I said that a snake had bitten him. But the cunning cyclist said, "How can there be so much of blood from a snake bite?" I made it up on the spur of the moment, saying that his foot had fallen on the tail of the snake, which bit him repeatedly and hence there was so much blood. In the hospital, the surgeon stitched Navin's foot and I returned home. After a month, when our classes restarted, Navin sat leaning to his left on his seat. Namita, who sat next to Navin, slapped him as he almost touched her. The teacher also shouted at Navin and asked him to sit properly. Later, perhaps she realised what could be the real problem with Navin and told him that he could not study in a normal school and he had better attend the school for specially-challenged children. Everyone in the class was stunned. It specially made me very angry, and I wanted to show my anger. I went to the Colonel's house. There on the signboard was written "Beware of the Dogs." I looked to my right and then to the left and rubbed off the letters inscribed on the name plate. Now, the sign board read: "Beware of the Dog." Dog, the Colonel!

CHAPTER 16

Backbencher (Humour)

(On the stage: Enter Dinu, Manu, Sheelu, Tenchi and Mantranath. They are all greatly surprised to see the New Campus)

Sheelu : Oh my God! How expensive this school looks to be!

Manu : Now, honestly speaking, I think our old campus was much better than this.

Dinu : Here, fees are four times higher, but books and teachers are the same, old as ever.

Sheelu : No, a no. Everywhere there are just tiles. Where shall we stick the chewing gum?

Dinu : Now, that we are here, let us take a round for inspection.

Manu : I have decided, fully finally and ultimately that I am not going to study here.

Sheelu : Hey, you Mantranath. Say something. It is you whose word will be the final.

Mantranath : Come, come. Let us move in and begin the inspection.

(At the end of the inspection)

Tenchi : A pity, really. We are backbenchers. So what?

Sheelu : This is not written on our foreheads. But what is eating you, Tenchi?

Tenchi : All of you are geniuses, all right. This bench is made of ply sheet. If Mantranath were to stand on it, all by himself, it would come crashing down.

Mantranath : Now here is my decision, I will not study here, nor anyone of you, for that matter.

Sheelu : Now, Mantranath easy. A fool you are and a fool you will remain. See, there is a lift, a swimming pool, a canteen, a fee room and the entire school is air-conditioned.

Mantranath : All right. I see your point, but there is one very big defect here. None of you seems to have noticed it. Such a huge building and yet there is no corner to hide. When we will bunk the class, where shall be hide?? See, what I mean! (All laugh)

CHAPTER 17

Self-respect versus Ego

Psychiatrist (Dr Jitendra's chamber)

Dr Jitendra : Yes, please. What is your problem?

Ghanshyam : This is my son, Lokesh. He always stands first in the class. But for the last two months, he has barely come out of his room, leave alone going to school.

(Dr Jitendra talks to Lokesh)

Dr Jitendra : Well Lokesh, how is your Papa with you? Does he beat you? Anything about him that you do not like?

(Lokesh nods his head in the negative)

Look Lokesh, please do not answer me with a nod. Say clearly, Yes or No. I am your uncle Chandan's friend. Now, answer me again.

Lokesh : My Papa is great!

Dr Jitendra : Does your mom take full care of you?

Lokesh : Dr Uncle, Mummy attends to even my smallest needs. I do not like it, but she even washes my clothes.

Dr Jitendra : And what about meals?

Lokesh : My Mummy is the best chef in the world.

Dr Jitendra : Tell me then, what happened in the school? Why do you refuse to go there?

Lokesh : Once Papa was away for a week from home for on official tour to Delhi and my 'Sir' had given me homework. It was the theorem of Pythagoras. He had instructed to come to the class fully prepared about the theorem. I could not understand the geometry of it. Papa was not at home. So I became a little careless.

Dr Jitendra : What happened after that?

Lokesh : Mishra Sir teaches Mathematics. He insulted me openly in the class before everyone. I could not answer his questions. In fact, I did not remember anything about Pythagoras and the theorem. I promised that I would learn it up by the next day, but Sir refused to listen to me.

(Dr Jitendra takes out a small pad and tears a sheet from it. Writes the name of Lokesh, his age and prescribes two tablets.)

Dr Jitendra : *(Addressing the parents of Lokesh)* Now, you must have realised his problem. Let him go to school and you better tell everything to Mishraji. What the teacher says, you will see, will put Lokesh at peace with him. It is a case of simple depression. Give this medicine, morning and evening for a couple of months. Everything will be all right.

Ghanshyam : Sir, the standard of the school is very high. How will I approach Mishraji to tell him my problem?

Dr Jitendra : However superior and high-class be the

schools and colleges, they can never be superior to the students.

SCENE 2

(Teacher's room)

Mishraji : So, Lokesh, how are you? Where did you disappear for two months? I was asking about you almost every day.

Ghanshyam : Sir, we went to a doctor yesterday. It was there that Lokesh disclosed everything. You had scolded him in the class before everyone. He took it very seriously and stopped even coming out of his room. Dr calls it depression. Actually, it was he who advised me to see you.

Mishraji : Oh! So this is it. How things have changed? When I was reading in the school, a single teacher taught us all the subjects. He was a good teacher and kind but when he taught mathematics, he would cane us. Later, he started using the cane for other subjects also. His canings sometimes left blue stripes on the skin. It hurt my body but never my soul. My self-dignity remained intact without any mark of injury. But now times are changing, so I also better change myself.

Lokesh : Sir, meanwhile, I have learnt everything about the theorem.

Mishraji : Good! From today you will sit in the front row.

CHAPTER - 18

Friendship – What a boon!

(A desolate air hangs over the drawing room of Maulana Anwar, who passed away only three days ago)

Anjum : Kasim, I have to say something to you.

Kasim : I am doing nothing, just idling! The mind is also wandering aimlessly. What a relief! Please do say something.

Anjum : Well, Maulana Abbu was 'destined to go'. People come only to go away.

Kasim : True. Death alone is permanent. You are a part of this house and a doctor also. You have taken good care of Abbu. I have also tried to serve him as best as I could.

Anjum : I have seen so many deaths in the medical college, but I have never ever thought that I would be watching my own Abbu, breathing out life slowly in my own lap till his pulse stopped beating.

Kasim : Till about the 9th April, he was almost normal. Only a little cough and mild fever.

Anjum : Cough and cold are so common, even at the age of 70. Nothing big about the fever also.

Kasim : Surely there was one big thing that he turned out to be Covid Positive. This Begum Pul of Meerut seemed kind of stuffed with medicine stalls and oxygen gas cylinders. There was a huge rush for remdesivir injections, almost as if some auction was being held for its purchases. By the way, how my friends whom you called idlers came in really handy at the hour of need!

Anjum : For the last three days, I had been insisting that we go to Delhi, where a friend of mine had arranged everything -- oxygen gas cylinders and beds. Everything was confirmed but Abbu would not agree.

Kasim : But from the fourth day onwards, Maulana Abbu was chanting nothing but Delhi, all the time. I do not know who had whispered what into his ears?

Anjum : Yes, I was also surprised, but was happy at the same time. A new ray of hope had kindled. I made him lie on the back seat of the car with his head resting on my lap.

(After sometime our car reached Ghaziabad)

Anjum : Abbu, we are in Ghaziabad. *(He opened his eyes and said to stop the car at Sharmaji's place)*

Kasim : Meeting Sharmaji will be just wasting time.

Anjum : Please do not say 'No' to anything that Abbu may say now. *(Kasim stopped the car at the pan stall of Sharmaji in Gumti).* I remember everything.

(As the glass shield of the door of the car was rolled down, Sharmaji moved briskly, offering a 'bida of pan' to Abbu. He carefully put it into his mouth after lowering the mask.)

Kasim : Maulana Abbu had given Sharmaji an envelope.

Anjum : Oh! Yes. Sharmaji's paan shop is just in front of our first factory.

Kasim : Maulana Abbu had also softly whispered something into Sharmaji's ears to take good care of the envelope and to tell his daughter that perhaps he might not be there for her marriage. Did you know what was in the envelope?

Anjum : I have a very faint recollection of all this. They were a lot of people going about here and there but I guess there must have been some money in it for Sharmaji.

(Anjum and Kasim are still talking when they are disturbed by the sound of a bell. Sharmaji enters the room. From his breast pocket the same envelope is peeping. Sharmaji takes Kasim into a close hug, while weeping bitterly with tears.)

Sharmaji : I was under the impression that Maulana must be in Delhi, but my neighbouring shop-owner told me everything and this is how I am here.

Kasim : But why are you returning this envelope?

Sharmaji : My son, Maulana, was a very dear and special friend of mine. I had been thinking for 40 years to remove my stall as it was marring the view of the factory. But I wanted to hear it from Maulana. I loved his words, whenever he spoke to me. He never ever mentioned about the shop. So, here we are. *(Still sobbing)*

Kasim : Do you know, Anjum, this is Abbu's will? It says the factory should be handed over to Sharmaji, after him.

(Kasim gently seats Sharmaji into the chair)

First of all, my apologies to you, Sharma Uncle. I could never fathom the depth of this friendship between you and Abbu.

Anjum : Uncle, this was Abbu's decision and no one can change it and one thing more: Whenever you come to Meerut, treat this bungalow as your own.

CHAPTER - 19

Round Table Conference (First)

Simon : Mr Prime Minister, this is my report, I mean the Simon Commission Report (May 1932).

Prime Minister (Ramsay MacDonald) : Simon, how do you see the future of the British Empire in India?

Simon : Conditions are not as they were. Gandhi has organised many movements. Now see, thousands of women, young and old people accompanied Gandhi for 340-km in the Dandi March. This march was led by the Congress with their Civil Disobedience campaign to make salt from the sea water.

Prime Minister : You man to say that in order to prolong the years of our rule in India, we should grant Indians some concessions also?

Simon : I hope the provincial elections will make some difference.

Prime Minister : You have very little experience. We have adopted the policy of divide and rule for the colonies.

Simon : In the other chamber of Prime Minister, they are waiting for you for the Round Table Conference.

(Both exit the room. On the stage are set

eight chairs with a table placed in the middle. All Indian delegates are present. With the entry of both His Majesty George V and the Prime Minister, all stand up).

His Majesty : I inaugurate this Round Table Conference and welcome all the delegates who have come from India.

Prime Minister : Look here! We regard all of you as our subjects. According to a study conducted under a royal charter, we wish to issue a proclamation for the people of India. We want you together under an All-India federal system with half the partnership in governments also. Now, you may say whatever you wish, one by one.

Garry : I am a British citizen but I am a member of the Congress. I have come to say that the Congress supports this Conference. Most of our leaders are in jail because of the Civil Disobedience Movement. This is why, even though willing, we are not participating in this Conference. (Leaves the room)

Mohammad Ali Jinnah (Muslim League): My party, the Muslim League, is against the federation as suggested by you. If we are denied power, we shall demand partition of India. We want a new country -- Pakistan.

M.R. Jaykar (Hindu Mahasabha): Sir, if Mr Jinnah so wishes, we do not contest him. Muslims may separate.

Sir Tej Bahadur Sapru (Liberal): Mr Jinnah, your two-nation theory is not acceptable to us. Gandhiji is not here. Do not try to take undue advantage of his absence.

Kailash Narain Haksar (Diwan of Gwalior): Sir, on behalf of the princely states of India, let me make it clear that our assets and our territories are not subject to the control of any political party. We do not support the Hindu Mahasabha and the Muslim League as well as the Congress.

B.R. Ambedkar : Sir, I have acquired 26 degrees from the universities in London, Chicago, France and Germany. Also, I am a Hindu. Only in name, though. Other Hindus treat us as untouchables. We cannot take water from their tanks and wells to drink. We cannot enter their temples to worship. If by chance, our cattle stray into their fields, they rain lathi-blows on the whole family. And surprise, surprise! Here in London, when I was doing my PhD, my roommate was a Hindu prince. We, therefore, ask for separate representation. This will be doing a great favour to the Dalit Community, which we are. This fact cannot be overlooked.

(At the end of the Conference, Prime Minister Ramsay Macdonald departs)

CHAPTER - 20

Gandhi-Irwin Pact

(New Delhi, March 2, 1931)

(On the stage: Viceroy Lord Irwin and Lt. Governor John Samuel are talking)

John Samuel : Lord, are we not giving too much importance to these blacks?

Irwin : It will take you some time, Samuel to understand what the British Government thinks. If Gandhi and other Congressmen don't attend the Second Round Table Conference, we shall fail. We have got to sign this Gandhi-Irwin Pact.

(On the stage, Gandhi and Sapru are talking)

Tej Bahadur Sapru: Bapu! If we want, we can talk about Bhagat Singh.

Gandhiji : Hang on Sapru, hang on! I have also suffered a lot. For years, I have been in jails. My fasts have broken the English. I have never apologised, nor have I ever committed violence.

Sapru : All right, I will not talk about it again.

Gandhiji : I can appreciate the sentiment of the people. But after the Chauri-Chaura violence, I withdrew the Non-cooperation Movement. I am no Mahatma. I am

Mohandas Karamchand Gandhi who supports non-violence and dislikes violence. That is all! *(Drinks water)*

Sapru : All right. Fine. So be it!

Gandhiji : This is the first time that the British Government has bent before the Congress. It is going to sign an agreement on the basis of equality. We are thus achieving a major objective.

(On the stage: Gandhiji and Viceroy Lord Irwin sign two documents separately and hand them over to Tej Bahadur Sapru and Lt. Governor John Samuel respectively. Both read the documents before a mike, turn by turn.)

Tej Bahadur Sapru: *(Reading out)* The British Government hereby declares the release of all political prisoners immediately except those who are accused of violence. The Indians can protest before shops selling foreign-made liquor and foreign clothes. People, who resigned from their posts during the movement, are hereby reinstated. Confiscated properties of agitators will be returned to them. Ninety thousand prisoners will be released from jails.

John Samuel : *(Reads out)* The Civil Disobedience Movement is being suspended. The Congress will take part in the Second Round Conference. The Congress will not boycott foreign goods. Gandhiji will withdraw his demand for inquiry into excessive injustice committed by the police.

CHAPTER - 21

Round Table Conference (Second)

(September-December 1931)

(According to the Gandhi-Irwin Pact, a delegation of the Congress under the leadership of Gandhiji has reached London to take part in the Second Round Table Conference. Gandhiji is accorded a grand welcome. Londoners waited for hours to catch a glimpse of him.)

Ramsay MacDonald: On behalf of His Majesty George V and the British Government, I welcome all parties and delegates to this Second Round Table Conference. The main objective of the Conference is that we want to give India a federal structure of the government. We also want to make some political changes to make India prosperous.

Gandhiji : Let me tell my friend Prime Minister Ramsay MacDonald that the All-India Congress Committee represents the whole of India. I am confident that you should please trust us and allow the Congress to function.

Madan Mohan Malviya: Mr Prime Minister, you must realise that with the Gandhi-Irwin Pact, Bapu has made his intentions very clear to all of you.

Jinnah : Mr Prime Minister, let me state to you clearly that the Muslim League is not in agreement with the Congress representation at all.

Maharaja of Bikaner: Honourable Prime Minister, on behalf of the different Indian states may I say that we do not recognise any political party. We want our princely states, our properties and our territories to remain intact.

M.R. Jaykar : Honourable Prime Minister, I am from the Hindu Mahasabha. India is a country of the Hindus. We oppose both the Congress and the Muslim League. We have ruled India for 5,000 years and shall continue to do so in the future.

B.R. Ambedkar : Honourable Prime Minister, I have obtained 26 degrees after studying in India, London, Chicago and France, with proficiency in finance and law specially. While I was completing my thesis in Chicago, my room partner for three years was from an Indian royal family. He was a prince and a great friend of mine. However, when I landed in British India with all my degrees, I became an untouchable, all of a sudden. Our residential areas where we stay are separate. We cannot draw water from their wells. We cannot go to the temples with them. Under such conditions, the Congress can never represent us. Let me state it, yet once again, that the Congress can never represent us. We, Dalits, represent ourselves!

Prime Minister : After so many differences, Mr Gandhi, do you realise that there is no communal harmony in your country. Amidst such hatred, this Round Table Conference comes to its end without any result.

CHAPTER - 22

Poona Pact

(September 24 1932)

(Stage: Yarvada Jail where, sitting, Gandhiji is reading a newspaper. Enter Pandit Madan Mohan Malviya and Rajendera Prasad.)

Rajendra Prasad : Bapu, as you had feared, so have the English acted!

Malviya : On the proposal of Ambedkar, in the Round Table Conference, Prime Minister Ramsay MacDonald has declared a Communal Award.

Gandhiji : I have also been informed that the English have allowed me a newspaper in the morning. Now, the Dalits will have two votes. Ambedkar was able to satisfy the Prime Minister. Actually, this is a ploy to postpone independence.

Rajendra Prasad : With their votes, the Dalits will now not only take part in general elections, they will also be able to elect their own representatives.

Gandhiji : It means that the candidate will be a Dalit and the voters will also be Dalits only.

Malviya : I remember. Bapu, you had opposed this proposal in writing before the Prime Minister.

Gandhiji : Now, since there is no solution at present, I am thinking of going on a fast unto death right from this moment.

Rajendra Prasad : No, Bapu, you do not have to go on such a fast. Your health is already down. We both will try to persuade Mr Ambedkar.

Gandhiji : Please do not worry about me. It's very hard to convince Ambedkar while he holds all the winning cards!

(Rajendra Prasad and Madan Mohan Malviya depart)

(Gandhiji is lying. He has been fasting for four days. Meanwhile, enter both Rajendra Prasad and Madan Mohan Malviya.)

Rajendra Prasad : Bapu, no need of fasting now. Ambedkar would be arriving in a while to sign a pact.

Malviya : Please, break your fast. Sip a little water.

Gandhiji : Do not worry so much for my sake. I will wait till Ambedkar arrives.

(B.R. Ambedkar enters)

Ambedkar : People have pressurised me too much because of your fast. If Dalits must sacrifice to save your life, so be it. I give up.

Rajendra Prasad : Bapu, in our pact, Mr Ambedkar will renounce the Communal Award in favour of joint electorate *(as it exists)*. As a result, 71 reserved seats under the Communal Award will be abolished for an overall increase in reserved seats to 148. Also, a fixed amount will be payable to the untouchables in every province on account of their education.

Malviya : There is now guarantee of recruitment of Dalits in the government services without discrimination. Please, both of you sign this agreement. It will be known as the Poona Pact.

(After the signing of the Poona Pact, Rajendra Prasad offers orange juice to Gandhiji to drink)

Ambedkar : Gandhiji, I have signed the Poona Pact with tears in my eyes to end the controversy, but for depriving the untouchables of their political rights and for exerting pressure on us to withdraw our demands, I call your fast unto death a drama.

CHAPTER 23

Social Reformer, Sir Syed Ahmed Khan

Born: October 17, 1817, New Delhi

Death: March 27, 1898, Aligarh

Education: Anglo Arabic School, Delhi

Founding of AMU: Conferred University Status as per 1920 AMU Act in 1921. It is believed to have been established on the Cambridge University model.

SCENE 1

(On the stage, two young men in Muslim dress)

Person No.1 : Sir Syed Ahmad Murdabad.

Person No. 2 : British Government Murdabad.

(Meanwhile, Sir Syed appears on the stage)

Sir Syed : You may issue a Fatwa against me, for my actions and my intent. Call me a subordinate of the English, if you like, but please pause for a moment and look at what I have been doing. The first thing that I did -- I opened a madarsa in Moradabad and afterwards, Gulshan School in 1859 and then opened a madarsa (which turned into Victoria School) in Ghazipur in 1863, and finally established the Mohammedan Anglo Oriental College in Aligarh in 1875. Very strange! Really? Our Hindu brothers have approved of my activities. I don't care. Call me names. Fellows, have pity on your young generation. Send them to schools. You will otherwise repent. I have spread my sheet before the public for donation. Gentlemen, donate liberally for education in English, Maths and Science.

SCENE 2

(Sir Syed appears on the stage as an IDEA)

Sir Syed : I had departed from this world in 1898 itself with dreams in my eyes. People considered me to be a henchman of the English. The British Government was my employer. Starting from Delhi, I ended up as sub-judge in Banaras. Later when I toured England, I was greatly impressed with the universities of Cambridge and Oxford there. However, I had to wait until 1920 to have a university for my qaum (community). (The Aligarh Muslim University took a constitutional shape in 1921 as per the 1920 AMU Act). I thank all my well-wishers and those young people of the Oxford University, who helped in the foundation of the AMU. I am also grateful to Hathras' Raja Mahendra Pratap Singh who did a big favour to the budding generation of Indians by donating "a good portion of land" for the university.

(Sir Syed Ahmad's form gradually moves out of the stage)

SCENE 3

(AMU V-C and others waiting with garlands of flowers on the stage on February 20, 1949 for the chief guest, Maulana Abul Kalam Azad. He enters the stage and is garlanded with thunderous clapping.)

Presenter : I earnestly request the first education minister of free India, Maulana Abul Kalam Azad, to please come to the mike.

Maulana Azad : I am grateful to the Vice-Chancellor, our brilliant professors and lecturers as well as the new generation, for inviting me on such an important occasion. Our countrymen will remain indebted to Sir Syed Ahmad Khan of the last century who had already foreseen the Aligarh Muslim University. Let us carry it forward -- I and you. As education minister, I promise the maximum assistance by the government (loud-clapping in the hall). Let me also share with you the views of Gandhiji about Sir Syed. He had said that Sir Syed was the modern prophet of education. When Pandit Nehru had visited the AMU, he had called this institution a symbol of our plural culture, what is known as the "Ganga Jamuni Tahzib".

CHAPTER 24

Kheda Agitation (February 1918)

(On the stage, lamenting farmers and Gandhiji enter)

Gandhiji : I know, you people are in trouble -- tell me everything in full detail.

Farmer 1 : It has not rained the whole year. There is no arrangement for water. Not even one fourth of the crop has survived.

Woman 1 : In this situation, how do we pay tax, Gandhiji?

Farmer 2 : The government is not willing to listen to us. The cattle and the children -- both are hungry. Tell me Sir, what shall we do?

Woman 2 : All our efforts and prayers have been in vain. You are a great man, Gandhiji. Show us the way.

Gandhiji : Look at this young man with me. He is Vallabhbhai Patel. He has given up his law practice. There will be Satyagrah (civil resistance) here named as the Kheda Satyagrah. Now, I seek your permission to leave. I have to go on a country-wide tour. Vallabhbhai will answer all your questions.

(Gandhiji leaves)

Vallabhbhai Patel : My brother farmers and sisters; Satyagrah means we don't have to pay any land revenue. All farmers, big and small, will follow it. In retaliation, the English can forcibly take away our land, our cattle and our household goods. But note one thing: We have to keep our Satyagrah non-violent. There should not be even a hint of force or violence in our protest.

(Shows a register) All peasants will have to sign a pledge on this paper (The English have started confiscating fields, cattle and other properties)

Farmer 1 : Patel Sir, they are seizing our other fields also illegally.

Patel : Mohanlal, go and pull the plants from their roots in the fields, which the English are trying to seize illegally.

(When Mohanlal moves, the English arrest him)

Patel : *(To the English)* You cannot arrest him. Do not give empty threats of firing and jail. Try it elsewhere. I know my law more than you do.

Boomfield : Yes, we can see how much law you know.

Patel : I have my law degree from London. You can try your utmost to shake my resolve.

Maxwell : All right. We are suspending tax-realisation.

(Gandhi Zindabad, Patel Zindabad, Satyagrah Zindabad -- slogans echo in the air)

CHAPTER - 25

Bardoli Satyagrah (June 1928)

SCENE 1

(On the stage: Three persons are sitting. All three are lawyers and busy in their legal work in the Ahmedabad Court. Advocate Vallbhbhai Patel is reading a newspaper.)

A lawyer : What is the news, Patel?

Patel : Here it says that the English are crossing all limits in Bardoli. Farmers are very angry.

Second lawyer : There is not much work for today. Tomorrow is a holiday. I say let us go to Bardoli. You agree?

(All three leave for Bardoli)

SCENE 2

(Some peasant women and men are sitting on the boundary of a field -- Patel talking to them)

Patel : I am Vallabhbhai Patel. All three of us are lawyers.

Lawyer 1 : You know Vallabhbhai has studied law in London.

Lawyer 2 : For us, Gandhiji is our role model. By the

way, what are your problems?

Farmer : Now what to say? All was going well until this English government increased the land tax by 30%, all of a sudden.

Patel : You need not worry. Now, we are all together in it. You had better call all the farmers for a talk. We will follow the path of Satyagrah as shown by Gandhiji. The name of our agitation will be 'Bardoli Satyagrah'.

(The crowd of peasants comes up close to the stage. Revenue Officer Maxwell and Regulating Officer Boomfield are in conversation with Patel.)

Patel : You have increased the tax from 6.03% to 30%, just in one go! All the peasants are opposing it vehemently. We have decided, I mean all of us are determined, that we will not deposit the increased tax.

Boomfield : We will dispatch you all to jail. Firing is also possible.

Patel : Yes. We are ready for jail and face your bullets. But we will not pay that tax.

(Boomfield and Maxwell talking together)

Maxwell : Okay, Mr Patel, you may pay tax at the old rate of 6.03 per cent.

(Maxwell issues orders in writing. The peasants hoist Patel on their shoulders and women, then and there, confer the title of 'Sardar' on Vallabhbhai Patel. There are slogans in the name of SARDAR Vallabhbhai Patel.)

CHAPTER - 26

Do Not be Provoked – Keep Your Cool /Do not get irritated (Humour)

(Two young boys arguing with each other and coming to blows. Meanwhile, enters an uncle.)

Uncle : Children, why are you fighting? What has happened to cause this?

Om : Uncle, leave us alone. This is between the two of us. Please do not get into it.

Hari Om : You want to know the facts, correct? Shall I say what was said?

Om : No, please no. Uncle will become angry. If you still want to say, go ahead.

Uncle : Look, I am a very cool person. You can share your problem with me. Tell me, what is it?

Hari Om : Uncle! This Om is very naughty. He teases me. Please say what should I do?

Uncle : Very simple! In life, if someone teases you, just refuse to be teased.

Om : Uncle, this is exactly what I say to Hari Om. Why do you get irritated? But his irritation shoots up so high that he comes down to fight. It is so easy to provoke him and then he will provoke the other person, and thus a quarrel begins.

Uncle : But son, you must refuse to be provoked.

Once there was a Mahatma...

Hari Om : Uncle, if someone teases you now, will you not feel annoyed?

Uncle : *(Assuming a pose).* Why should I feel bad? I am not going to be provoked come what may!

Hari Om : If someone were to call you a mug; I mean a 'kullad', won't you feel bad about it?

Uncle : No, why should I? And a mug matters little to me.

Hari Om : But your face, Uncle, tells a different story. You are feeling bad, clearly, though you are claiming that calling mug has not hurt you.

Uncle : You know it. I am the president of the colony. Get lost. I am a doctor also and I can give you the 'needle treatment'. Injection, you see?

Om : Hari Om, leave Uncle, for God's sake. Otherwise, he may start pulling his hair. Let us move.

Uncle : Insulting someone like this? It is not done. Give me your addresses; I will speak to your fathers.

(Om and Hari Om laugh. Address, you said.)

(Both them try to mimic a beer mug with their hands)

Hari Om : You were the 99th target. Let us see who comes within the range, tomorrow?

(Take to their heels – and run away)

CHAPTER - 27

English Quit India

(Quit India Movement)

(8 August, 1942, Tardeo Bombay)

(All leaders are sitting on the stage. The people are standing in the back and on the road. English soldiers are keeping a strict vigil.)

Sucheta Kriplani : We are lucky that Gandhiji along with his dedicated and able leading followers is himself present. Today, the central point under discussion will be Gandhiji's proposal – English Quit India. I will invite first, the nightingale of India, Sarojini Naidu, who is guiding Bengal and South India.

Sarojini Naidu : Respected Mahatma Gandhi, Mr President and leaders, when Lord Curzon had divided Bengal in 1905 on communal basis, it was time for his exit. Now is the time for the English to Quit India. I am in full agreement with the proposal and I support it.

Sucheta : Now, I invite the leader from the United Provinces, Pt. Jawaharlal Nehru, who is an apple of the eye of the youth.

Nehru : The English, till today, have not made any proposal that might be acceptable.

The Indian National Congress had opposed the British even before the arrival of Mahatma Gandhi in India from South Africa. Opposition is always there. Voices were raised against the partition of Bengal, against the Rowlatt Act, Crips Mission, Jallianwala Bagh and so on. After the Chauri Chaura episode, Mahatma Gandhi had withdrawn the Non-cooperation Movement. We will have to conduct our movement along the line of non-violence and love. I support this proposal.

Sucheta : Now, Maulana will express his views.

Maulana Abul Kalam Azad: The Muslim League, Bhartiya Hindu Mahasabha and even Mohammad Ali Jinnah have opposed the Quit India Movement and this meeting here. The stone blocks of Yervada Jail, the Naini Jail, and in fact a dozen more such jails in the country, bear the imprints of our backbones on them. Gandhiji himself has been a jail inmate for years. I was born on the holy land of Islam in Mecca and now the secret soil of India is my scene of action. Having studied Arabic, Urdu, Hindi, Sanskrit and English, I have come to conclusion that the path showed by Gandhiji -- that is freedom and it is the right course for us. None is more tolerant than the Hindus. I am totally against Mohammad Ali Jinnah and the Muslim League's two-nation theory. Muslims cannot be safer anywhere other than India. The Non-cooperation Movement or Civil Disobedience, both are in accord with basic Islamic principles. The method of the Gandhian protest is the right one. Few extremist Hindus and Muslims are opposing Gandhiji. They call him half-naked fakir. They do not understand him. This grand old man is showing us the way to follow. I support the Quit India Movement.

Sucheta : Now, I request the presence of Shri Patel on the stage.

Patel : We have to make the dream of Gandhiji a reality. The Congress has always been against the policy of persecution and torture of freedom fighters. We have to bring together some 545 Indian States, big and small to make the country: One United India. This countless crowd in the Gwaliya Tank Park is looking at us with hopeful eyes for freedom. I wish to convince them that braving the stormy waves of the ocean, our boat of freedom is very close to the shore. However, Mr Jinnah, his Muslim League, the Indian Communist Party and Hindu Mahasabha have not joined our Quit India Movement even after written requests. Many big leaders have gone underground. I support Gandhiji's proposal.

Sucheta : Now, Mahatma Gandhi will express his views. (Gandhiji enters amidst lusty cheers and slogans of the English Quit India -- Angrezon Bharat Chodo.

Gandhiji : (With folded hands, appeals to the people to be quiet) My friends, I have not changed at all since 1920. Today, the world is shedding blood for the sake of freedom. But God has given me a weapon of non-violence which is the most powerful. Owing to Nehruji I had studied the Soviet Model to acquire freedom and I have found that in order to achieve that there should be unity among Hindus and Muslims. We should not hate the English. Many of them are my friends. We do not dislike people. We dislike the British Government and their cruel laws and the way they are looting India. Violence leads to autocracy. Non-violence will get us freedom and democracy. After Independence, the people will decide who will rule the country.

The Second World War has turned the earth red. The people are shedding blood and tears to be free. We should learn to live in love with one another, forgetting the differences of caste, colour and creed. I entreat Indians, who oppose independence, and favour the British to join this non-violent movement of "English Quit India" and tell it to the whites that their time in India is over. They had better go home. They are not welcome here anymore. *(Slogans of Mahatma Gandhi Zidabad, Do or Die, Quit India... fill the air. The police arrive. There are arrests and confusion. Suddenly, Aruna Asaf Ali unfurls and waves tiranga, the tri-colour)*

CHAPTER - 28

Annie Besant

(Born: October 1, 1847, London)
(Died: September 20, 1933, Madras)

Presenter : This is the Banaras Hindu University. It was at this Ghat in 1933 that the ashes of Annie Besant were immersed, as per her wish, in the Holy Ganga. By name she was Christian, but spiritually she was Hindu to the core. Behind me is the Banaras Hindu University. Along with Pt. Madan Mohan Malviya, Sunderlal and other Indian princes, Annie Besant was also the founder member. She came to India in 1893. She was India's first Iron Lady. She blew the bigul (bugle) of Independence for India and Ireland. In 1918, Bal Gangadhar Tilak started the Swarajya or Home Rule Movement. Annie Besant and Tilak together designed a flag for the Home Rule Movement.

A great orator and organiser, Annie Besant was a socialist and a spiritual writer. Opposing injustice ran in her blood and she was a great supporter of women's rights.

(Now let's go to the all India Congress Session, Calcutta, 1917)

(On the stage with others: Pandit Madan Mohan Malviya and Annie Besant. A woman

behind the mike conducts the meeting and requests Pandit Mandan Mohan Malviya, who is also the president for the session, to address the meeting.)

Malviya : I just want to announce that today I complete my term as president of the Congress and that for the first time a lady is going to succeed me. I mean Annie Besant. (She is garlanded on the stage by Congress members) Now, I request the new Congress president to express her views.

Annie Besant : I gratefully acknowledge the honour that Malviyaji has given me. This is a proof of moral courage of the Congress that it has made me the president. I am a London-born white woman and I am here to fight the English government for India's independence. When I came to India in 1893, I saw a great similarity between Irish and the Indian struggle for self-government. I consider India my motherland, with my heart, soul and body.

The Congress is an organisation, which is fighting against injustice. As you know, the Home Rule Movement was first born in Ireland. It means the right of a country to make its own laws and rules of governance.

Now, I will request Pandit Madan Mohan Malviya and respected Tilakji to persuade Gandhiji to join the Congress and clear the way for our campaign to move forward. There is only one way to Freedom and that is Mahatma Gandhi.

(Slogans Annie Besant Zindabad, Mahatma Gandhi Zindabad echo in the air)

CHAPTER - 29

Begum Hazrat Mahal

(Born: 1820, Faizabad)

(Died: 1879, Kathmandu, Nepal)

(1857, India's First War of Independence, Lucknow)

Maid Servant : Begum Sahiba, heir apparent to the throne and the new King of Awadh, Birjis Kadar, is arriving.

Begum : *(Hugs her son)* We are grateful to Emperor Bahadur Shah for his kindness in recognising your status and sending two gold coins *(asharfis)* as a token of goodwill.

Birjis : Ammi Jaan, cruelties of the English are multiplying.

Begum : You sit on the throne. I will take care of Awadh.

Maid : Begum, Sir Henry Lawrence from the Residency has come.

Henary : Begum, Queen Victoria in London wants a treaty of friendship with you.

Begum : What does she want in return?

Henary : The whole of Awadh will be yours once again, but the rule will be of the British. The Union Jack will continue to flutter on the Residency.

Begum : Go and tell your Queen that we will blast the residency with cannons and gun powder.

Henary : Begum, you know. You cannot do it.

Begum : If anything happens to Emperor Bahadur Shah, we will make Residency a graveyard.

Henary : Begum, you are very angry, but who does not know that you are from Faizabad…

Begum : *(Stands up in a huff)* Now get lost. I know you have called Major Hudson from Delhi.

(Begum Hazrat Mahal laid a siege at the Residency with her army, Zamindars and mixed groups of Hindus and Muslims. The three-story structure collapsed. Major Hudson found out and surrounded by Begum's soldiers was killed in the Begum Kothi locality. It was the same Major Hudson who had presented to Bahadur Shah Zafar the heads of two of his sons and one great grandson on a plate covered with a red scarf. A local Hindu Zamindar managed to send the Begum to Nepal, Kathmandu, where she died in 1879.)

CHAPTER - 30

Royal Family (Humour)

(On the stage: Begum enters accompanied by a maid servant)

Begum : I say, where has Nawab Saheb gone?

Maid : Must be around. Somewhere, here only. Where else will he go?

Begum : The paandaan *(betel box)* is with me. Without the paan his throat must be parching!

Maid : Oh! See. Here he is sitting.

Begum : What are you doing here, Nawab Saheb?

Nawab : Just peeling this blessed orange!

Begum : Oh My God! Save us from trouble. Three hours have gone and not even half the orange is peeled.

Nawab : What do you know? How many fibres are there in an orange?

Begum : It just takes two minutes. Now, you will give me lesson in peeling oranges.

Nawab : Doctors say that a single orange fiber, if it sticks in the teeth, can cause cancer!

Begum : My dear, here is the paandaan. You will need another three to four hours perhaps to peel the orange. I am off to the exhibition. We shall meet there. I will be waiting.

Nawab : Okay.

(Nawab Saheb sitting in a chair comfortably and busy peeling the half-peeled orange)

Chowkidar : Sir, will you now please move from here?

Nawab : What? And may I know who are you?

Chowkidar : Sir, I am the Chowkidar.

Nawab : I have no objection to it, but why should I move?

Chowkidar : It is time, Sir, to lock up the hall. Better hurry Sir.

Nawab : No. No, by all means. Begum has told me to meet here only. See, what would happen, if she comes and am not here.

CHAPTER - 31

Lord Buddha

SCENE - 1

(On the stage: Royal astrologer and King Shuddhodhan, talking among themselves)

King : Astrologer Sir, now that you have seen my son, please forecast his future.

Astrologer : In the time to come, your son will be a great king, ruler of a big kingdom or else…

King : Why have you stopped? Please complete your forecast.

Astrologer : But moved with sorrow and death, he will take 'Sanyas' *(renunciation)* and distance himself from princely life.

King : You mean because of the pain and troubles of others -- no, I will not let him become a monk *(Sanyasi)*.

Astrologer : *(Bows his head with folded hands)* now I want to leave.

King : Go! And bring Army Chief Kaushal. Immediately.

(King looking into some official papers. Meanwhile, the Army Chief arrives on

the stage.)

Army Chief : Awaiting orders, Sir! Looking worried, but why, my Lord?

King : I am putting the prince under your care. Watch out! He should never be out of the palace.

SCENE - 2

(16 YEARS LATER)

Siddharth : Look here. I am now a grown up adult and I wish to go out of the palace.

Army Chief : Right, Siddharth. Here I take you out!

(A view of out the palace)

Siddharth : *(Seeing an old man in front)*

Chief, who is he and why is he looking like this?

Army Chief : Siddharth, when someone grows up in age, he becomes old. His body organs do not function properly. This is called old age.

Siddharth : Chief, come! Who is he and what has happened to him?

Army Chief : He is a young man. There are several wounds on his body. This is why he is crying in pain. And the pain is so much that he cannot bear it.

Siddharth : *(Thinking)* All right! Come now! Who are these four persons carrying another in a lying posture?

Army Chief : These four persons are carrying the dead body of a person for cremation because his life is now over and done with.

(As if a mountain of sorrow has crashed upon Siddharth. He talks to himself in a pensive mood. How can the world be saved from old age, pain and death? He is lost in deep thought... How?)

Siddharth : All right, then! I am going to leave this palace, my father Shuddhodhan, aunt Gautami, wife Yashodhara and son Rahul. I will leave, today itself and go into the forest to seek salvation from all these problems.

(Looking to his right and left, Siddharth departs from the stage)

(An unseen voice from a distance)

(In the centre of the stage under a peepal tree is sitting Siddharth, cross-legged and doing penance. He achieves Enlightenment (Gyan) in the 35th year of his life and is known as Buddha.)

Principal teachings of Buddha –

1. Buddha Agnihotra and Gayatri Mantra.
2. Meditation and introspection.
3. Follow the middle course in life.
4. Four cardinal truths
5. Ashtang method.

I, Buddha, pass on this message to my followers that they take to the path of non-violence and truth -- today, this date, this hour, I declare the birth of a new religion: Buddhism, the Bauddha Dharma. And thus he came to be regarded as Bhagwan (God).

CHAPTER – 32

Rani Laxmi Bai

Born: November 19, 1828
Place of birth: Assi Ghat, Kashi
Died: June 18, 1858; Kota Sarai, Gwalior

"Every Bundela mouth has one story to tell, Man-like, this Rani of Jhansi fought and fighting she fell" (*Bundele harbolon ke munh hamne Suni kahani thi, khoob ladi mardani woh to Jhansi wali rani thi*)

Presenter : We have heard from every Bundela mouth, the tale of Rani of Jhansi. How man-like she had fought a fierce battle! (*Bundele harbolon ke munh hamne Suni kahani thi, khoob ladi mardani woh to Jhansi wali rani thi*) You may have heard these stirring words of the poetess Subhadra Kumari Chauhan.

"I the childhood friend of the Rani Nilima Dhulekar will tell you about that 1857 warrior, Laxmi Bai. Rani's father, Moropant Tambe, worked in the court of Peshwa of Bithoor. His daughter Manikarnika was born on the Assi Ghat in Kashi. She was an expert in religious texts and use of arms, horse-riding and swordsmanship. She was married to the Maratha King of Jhansi, Gangadhar Rao, in 1842. After marriage, her childhood name Chabili-Mani was changed to Laxmi Bai.

SCENE - 1

Raja : Look here, Rani! I have brought you to this highest platform in the fort so that you may get a bird's eye-view of the entire kingdom.

Rani : Wonderful. Very beautiful.

Raja : Here is this Betwa River, flowing as a witness to several Maratha kingdoms. To the east is the Khajuraho temple where our people are going to pray.

Rani : The climate of this place is very warm.

Raja : This is the reason that not only in Jhansi, but in the whole of Bundelkhand, there are huge rocks of stone under a thick layer of soil.

Rani : But the people are gentle in speech, honest and industrious. This is all because of you. This is why Jhansi is developed.

Raja : Far distant is the palace of the Orchha Bundelas. There, out of friendship with Salim (Mughal Emperor Jahangir), Raja Rajvir Singh had built a palace to welcome him.

Presenter : After marriage, the Rani gave birth to a son but he was alive for four months only. To get over the blow of his son's death, the Raja had adopted Damodar Rao as his son. But in 1853, the king also died. With one voice, the courtiers put the 4-year old adopted son on the throne.

SCENE - 2

(The courtiers are present in the royal court. All stand up when the Rani enters. Rani signs them to take their seats.)

Rani : You know the reason for this emergency meeting of the Jhansi Raj Darbar? The British Government has declared the coronation of our adopted son illegal under the "Doctrine of Lapse".

Peshwa : But this is against our Maratha tradition.

Ghulam Gaus Khan: Let the English give such threats to others!

Dewan Jawahar : The whole country is opposing the policies of the British Government.

Rani : Lord Dalhousie has made a proposal that for Rs 60,000 per year, the rule of Jhansi should be handed over over to the British. Gaus Khan, you are the closest to our Maratha royal dynasty. Tell us: "What are your plans?"

Ghulam Gaus Khan: The Jhansi Darbar is in deep trouble. The whole country is in turmoil. Now, the time has come to leave the court and turn to the cannon, Kadak-Bijli, against the British. This is the hour of gunpowder and revolt.

Rani : I expected as much from you. Come what way, I am not going to give away my Jhansi.

(Victory to Rani Laxmi Bai – Jay, Raj Darbar Ki Jay. No, no, no! Victory to the people of Jhansi.)

Presenter : After this secret decision by the court of Jhansi, in June 1858, the army of Jhansi, under the leadership of Rani Laxmi Bai, and the British forces came face to face. The battle lasted for about 15 days with the English suffering many reverses. Meanwhile, the revolt of 1857 was in full bloom all over India. The army of Rani was battling the British. In a book, one Captain Rodrick says that he had seen Rani Laxmi Bai in action very closely. She was robust in built and had beautiful eyes with a round face. At that time, Rani was holding the reins of the horse with her teeth and wielding the sword with both of her hands. In the meantime, a spear hit her in the chest. Rani cut the English into two but again a bullet pierced her body. The soldiers of Jhansi had taken the Rani into a protective circle. The wounded queen galloped away on her horse but when she spurred the stallion to jump across a gully, she failed, and suffered injuries. Even though she managed to escape from there, the fatally wounded Rani ultimately died on June 18, 1858 in a temple near Kota Sarai in Gwalior.

CHAPTER - 33

Search for Ashfaq!

[Some people are getting ready to offer namaz (prayers)]

Zarina : Mushtaq, are you folks going for Friday prayers?

Mushtaq : Yes, sister. Just across the grove is the mosque. Only last year, we had all made it 'pucca'.

Zarina : What! First, the houses should be pucca. Anyway Ashfaq is ready. Please take him along too.

(Ashfaq is aged 8)

(He accompanies his 'uncle'. All return after an hour. But Zarina is not able to locate her son for quite some time.)

Zarina : It is so late, Mushtaq. Ashfaq is not to be seen. He must also be hungry. Where is he?

Mushtaq : Do not worry, sister. It is a small village. I will just find and bring him to you.

(Mushtaq, along with some four-five persons, goes out to find Ashfaq. Mushtaq and his search party return.)

Zarina : Hey, why these long faces? Every one of you looks the same?

Mushtaq : I have searched the whole village -- the fields and among the harvest, everywhere. Nowhere has he been seen. Seems he is lost.

Zarina : He is not that simple. He cannot lose his way. Search again. Carefully. Search in the masjid also.

(All run towards the mosque)

(Ashfaq is sitting on the door-sill of the mosque and laughs at the sight of the search party)

Mushtaq : Everyone is looking for you. What are you doing here?

Ashfaq : But no one has given me prasad *(offering)*. I am waiting.

Mushtaq : Son, prasad is offered in temples, not in mosques.

(He picks up his nephew Ashfaq in his lap)

CHAPTER - 34

Netaji Subhash Chandra Bose

SCENE 1

Anil Majumdar : Netaji, today is 26 January. Last year, Pt. Jawaharlal Nehru had celebrated Independence Day with great enthusiasm in Lahore in spite of the opposition by the English.

Netaji : Yes, I remember it all. Perhaps you don't know. Today, we will celebrate it in Calcutta and hoist the flag also, with the same joy and fun as experienced by Nehruji. Only the frontier Gandhi will not be here -- I mean our Khan Abdul Ghaffar Khan.

Majumdar : If Mahatma were to unfurl the tricolour it would be like an icing on the cake!

Netaji : Now, come on, it is getting to be 10 o' clock. Let us hurry. There will be quite a crowd, when we host the flag.

(A large sportsfield. The crowd is shouting slogans of Subhash Chandra Bose and Mahatma Gandhi. The policemen are patrolling in uniform and plain clothes around thousands of people. There are also English police officers mounted

on muscular horses are also there as if some major incident is about to happen. Meanwhile, Netaji appears on the stage. Slogan shouting gets louder. An English soldier, flaunting a letter, declares the meeting illegal.)

Netaji : Friends! The English government has just informed me that this meeting and our flag-hoisting is against the law. I wish, however, to tell the government that calling a meeting and hoisting the flag is our birthright. I don't agree with the government's view. As Mahatma Gandhi says "you may beat us to your hearts", even take our life, if you want, on our part we shall not raise our hands to strike back.

(Subhash Chandra Bose tugs at the string of the flag)

Comrades, remember my slogan: Give me blood, I promise you freedom.

(Meanwhile, the police swoop down on the people from all sides. In no time, people are drenched in blood. Subhash Chandra Bose falls down under laathi blows. The police arrest Subhash Chandra Bose, Anil Majumdar, Robin Chatterjeea together with 150 other persons.)

SCENE - 2

Gandhiji : Mr Viceroy, you cannot beat and arrest any of our leaders like Bose!

Willingdon : Mr Gandhi, your young leader, Bose, has

broken the law. Our man had asked him in writing not to hoist the flag.

Gandhiji : If a person hoists his tricolour flag in his own country, how can it be called a crime?

Willingdon : Mr Gandhi, excuse me. I can do nothing on this written application of yours.

Gandhiji : I do not wish to waste your valuable time if you do not release all our prisoners. You will compel us to announce the launch of the Non-cooperation Movement. I hope that the Prime Minister of Britain will not lose his temper on you.

Willingdon : Mr Gandhi, I am afraid you have not understood me fully. What I am saying is that all your arrested leaders in Calcutta will be let off by tomorrow morning except Bhagat Singh and his violent companions.

Gandhiji : All right, Mr Viceroy. Thank you.

(Subhash Chandra Bose and his friends are freed)

Bose (on phone) : Our release does not matter. Please have Bhagat Singh, Sukhdev and Rajguru freed.

Gandhiji : I have stayed in jails, sat on hunger strikes but never apologised nor did we indulge in violence ever.

Bose : It might be all right for you but I disagree.

CHAPTER - 35

Poisoning

(Aboylyingunconsciousonahospitalbedforthelastthreedays. Things are serious. Medicines are being administered by injection.)

Dr Bhupendra : Look here, Nurse. The glucose must continue. I am going for an operation. If the boy gains consciousness, please inform me at once.

Nurse : All his post-investigation reports are normal, yet he has not regained senses. Why?

Doctor : Maybe there was poison in what he ate.

Nurse : Quite likely because the police took him down in an unconscious state from the Farrukhabad Mail. I think it is a case of poisoning.

Doctor : Poisoning? Why? The poor chap did not have even the smallest luggage with him. Why poison such a person?

Nurse : Doctor, he must have eaten something poisoned. Look, the mark around the wrist is there, but there is no watch. He was brought wearing a thin shirt without sweater. Someone must have taken away his sweater and luggage.

Doctor : Oh yes! I had read it somewhere that 13% of the cases of poisoning in the country take place in Kanpur. On one hand, we are famous for making attar in Kannauj, while on the other hand people poison passengers in trains for small gain.

Nurse : Oh, oh, Sir, the boy seems to be regaining his senses!

(The patient opens his eyes. Doctor pats his cheeks. The nurse washes his face. The boy sits up.)

Doctor : What is your name?

Patient : Gopal.

Doctor : And where do you live?

Patient : I live in Lucknow. Where am I, now?

Doctor : You are in a hospital in Farrukhabad.

Patient : Doctor Sahab, I had a suitcase with me. Where is it?

Nurse : Son, you have been senseless for the last three days. Today you have gained sense.

Doctor : How did it all happen? And what is your age?

Gopal : Doctor Saheb, I am 15. My elder sister is married in Farrukhabad where I was going. Oh yes, now I can recall. In Kayamganj, two uncles sat down in the vacant seat by my side. They were dressed differently. From a pocket one of them took out glucose biscuits, which first he ate and then gave to the other person. They also gave me a biscuit to eat. On my saying no, they insisted that I take at least one. It will do me good. I ate the biscuit and I am opening my eyes now.

Doctor : You are not going to Farrukhabad. You are there already.

Gopal : And my attache, and my sweater? Where are they?

Nurse : The biscuit you ate was poisoned. Never eat anything offered by a stranger. Elders of the house and even the government, through advertisements say the same thing. Thank God, your life is saved. *(Gopal begins weeping.)*

Gopal : There were 2,000 rupees in the bag, which my mother had given for my elder sister. Now, what shall I do?

Doctor : Son, you have committed a great mistake and you will have to pay for it. Do not eat anything given by a stranger in journey and nor indulge in business with anyone. Nurse, call the police for necessary legal action. Perhaps his attache might be recovered. Discharge him after the necessary paperwork.

CHAPTER - 36

Monitor (Humour)

(Classroom, 7th grade students are seated. In the front row are sitting Seema, Somesh, Subhash, Javed, Jyoti and Manju. Seating arrangement is according to the ability of the students.)

Ma'am : Children! This is your first day in the class. I welcome you, all. This is the A.M.C. branch of the Kendriya Vidyalaya, Lucknow. This school was started in 1963 especially for the children of army personnel by the Central Government. You may not be aware of my name. Well, it is Santhanam. Now introduce yourselves, I mean, tell your names.

Student 1 : My name is Seema.

Student 2 : My name is Somesh.

Student 3 : My name is Subhash

Student 4 : Ma'am I am Jyoti.

Ma'am : All right. Your introduction is done. Now, who would like to be the monitor from among you? Raise your hand.

(None of the students raise a hand)

So, no one wants to be the monitor? Seema, you say something.

Seema : These innocent looking mischief-mongers cannot be controlled by me. No way! Ma'am, I will not be the monitor!

Ma'am : Come on Subhash. If I correctly remember, your elder sister Nilima was once a student here?

Subhash : Ma'am, I study half the time and sing during the remaining half. As monitor, it is beyond me to collect the copies of all the students of the class.

Ma'am : What about you, Jyoti?

Jyoti : To be honest with you, Ma'am. No one will agree to be the monitor. This is what had happened in Class VI also. Tripathi Sir had then shouted at Ashok Maharaj and forced him to be the monitor, I mean against his wish. As it is, Ashok has to do nothing with studies.

Ma'am : Ashok, would you then be the monitor?

Ashok : Well, I had decided not to be a monitor but I also cannot rebut what Jyoti has said.

Jyoti : What is this rebuttal business? Within, you must be feeling puffed up. But remember one thing while collecting the copies that my copy should be the last to be collected. Will you get it, Maharaj?

Subhash : Ma'am, the school starts with the assembly. Monitor is excused from the assembly. One day when I asked my mummy to pack four "idlis" for my tiffin, she said "My son, I do pack four 'idlis'". Now, this is what I feel. Look Ashok, I am not naming you but it is during the assembly only that someone ate two of my idlis!

Ashok : Listen, Subhash. I am stating this before Ma'am. I have never stolen your 'idlis', like someone who polishes off an egg paratha from my tiffin. And now, listen, carefully. If you wish to eat four 'idlis' in tiffin, you had better bring six 'idlis' daily.

Ma'am : My! My! The whole lot of you. I do not mind all this. We teachers also eat up each others' tiffins. So what? Here, Ashok, you are duly "appointed" the monitor. And, one more thing children, once this student life is over, you will long for these days wistfully, all your life.

CHAPTER - 37

Galileo Galilei

(Born: February 15, 1564, Pisa city in Italy)

(Died: January 8, 1642, Arcetri city in Italy)

Father's Name : Vicenzo Galilee, a musician who played lute which later evolved as guitar and banjo.

SCENE 1

(Galileo is busy looking at articles spread on his table, like a lantern, a telescope, candle and other knick-knack. Enters father, playing the lute)

Father : *(Addressing the audience)* There was a time in Europe when Rome and Greece were in decline. The whole continent was lost in the darkness of ignorance. But darkness is always followed by light. Time took a turn. Progress in science and technology pulled Europe out of darkness, leading to light. The scientist who did the most was Galileo Galilei.

Galileo : Father, once again, you are disturbing me, and breaking my concentration.

Father : Do not be annoyed, Galo your mother

and I have given you birth and brought you to this earth *(laughs)*.

Galo : But father, it is not Sunday today. Do you doubt my intelligence?

Father : Who can I trust more than you, son? But I am somewhat shaken in my confidence about you.

Galo : Let me work, please. You better retire to your room.

Father : All right, then. I am going to sleep.

(While father leaves for his room, Galo suddenly leaps with joy)

Galo : Come. Come father. Let me show you something.

Father : What? What has happened?

Galo : I have the formula to measure the speed of light!

Father : All right, explain it to me.

Galo : Suppose, you are standing at the tallest eastern point of Pisa and I am on the tallest western point. If you light a lantern there, the time that light will take to reach me, the travelling time, is called the speed of light.

Father : I know it depends on one's commitment. If you have it, success is yours. *(Galo goes back to his work and father talks to the audience)*

Until an astronaut scientist, Oley Romer, correctly assessed the speed of light to be 3 lakh kilometers per second in 1676, Galileo's theory was considered to be the final truth.

SCENE - 2

(Galileo working till late in the night at his table)

Father : Astronomical research into the discovery of characters and mountains on the moon and all the four satellites of Jupiter will generally be known as Galileo's satellites.

(Galileo peers into the sky through his telescope)

He watches the various aspects of the Venus planet and found out in precise terms their speed by a study of solar sounds. Galileo came to the conclusion that Aristotle's global mapping theory was incorrect. On the other hand, he supported the solar-centric theory of Copernicus that the Sun was in the centre of the entire solar system. Now, let us see what follows next…

(Galileo is gazing at the sky intently with his telescope by changing his position frequently. He writes the analytical findings of the solar-centric theory in his diary on the table and refutes the long-established beliefs and what the religious texts say that the Sun goes around the earth and that the earth is static. My analysis, Galileo says, has proved everyone wrong. Let others think what they want. He has proved with his theory, for all time to come that the satellites, including the Earth -- which is a part of the solar system -- move around the Sun

only and not vice-versa. The Sun is static and the Earth revolves round it. The part of the Earth facing the Sun is lighted and the part away from the Sun remains dark. This is how days and nights occur.)

Galo : Father, come out of your room. (Father enters the stage)

Father : What is the matter? I was asleep.

Galo : See, what I have written in my note? *(Father reading the note)*

Father : What is all this? What rubbish have you written, Galo? You seem to know more than the heavenly Father, the God? You need to spend some time in a mental asylum. If it is published in the newspapers tomorrow that the Earth revolves around the Sun, as you say, what might happen? Can you estimate the repercussions?

Galo : Father, my theory is the most important for me. In fact, for every dweller on this Earth, I don't care for the consequences!

Father : You know it very well. In the Christians states, Church is supreme. The king and the royalty come second. My acquaintance with King Manuel is confined to my playing the lute to comfort him during the night as he finds it hard to sleep. In return, I get a few coins.

Galo : I do not agree with you. For me, there is only one and ultimate God.

SCENE - 3

(Open space where a priest is sitting on a chair. Below him is

sitting the king and the queen. In the crowd, in the front, stands Vicenza Galileo with hands tied, while a calm Galileo stands in an enclosure. There is a milling crowd around.)

Andrew : *(A young priest)*: Reverend Father, with your permission, shall I begin interrogation of the culprits?

Priest : *(In the chair)* Permission granted. Go ahead!

Andrew : Honourable Sir, this man standing in the enclosure is named Galileo Galilei. He has slandered the Holy Bible and other religious texts. He has challenged the Church. He says it's not the Earth, but the Sun that goes around the Earth. Our Holy Book, which has come down from the Heaven -- and no one doubts it -- says, and rightly, that the Earth is stationary. The entire solar system, including the Sun, moves around the Earth. Reverend Sir, it is also a fact, in his own way, Galileo is a great intellectual. He is an astronomer, a philosopher, mathematician, physicist and an inventor. This is what the society in Pisa thinks about him. Honourable Sir, now your decision is awaited.

Galileo : Sir, May I say something? *(The Priest indicates "yes" with his hand)*

Reverend Father and members of the Assembly, I would like to say that I am a faithful Christian and I have full faith in the Father in Heaven.

Priest : Prisoner in the enclosure, Galileo Galilei, if you have full faith, as you say, in the

Father in Heaven and the Holy Bible, you will have to admit that you are wrong. You must recant from your theory.

Andrew : Galileo, what are you thinking? The reverend priest has given you a chance to right your wrong. If you like, you can be set free with honour from this enclosure. Now, what do you have to say?

Galileo : Honourable Sir, the harshest punishment, which can be given, is death. I may be hanged tomorrow morning or whatever else the Lord Priest decides for me. Now, hear you all! I want to announce it, here and now in public that my discovery of the solar theory, after a serious study of the Sun through telescope, is neither against religion, nor it is wrong. I am not going to apologise or recant. Whatever punishment the Honoubale Priest gives is acceptable to me.

Priest : Galileo, you criminal! You want to modify the Bible? As long as Christianity lives, heretics like you will come and go but the Bible will go on forever. I take your theory to be a serious violation of Christianity and the Bible. I would have given you the maximum punishment but in view of your many services to your community, you are sentenced to imprisonment for life only. Oh yes, there is this exception: You will complete your sentence under detention in your own house.

(The Priest stands up and leaves)

CHAPTER - 38

Charles Darwin

(Theory of Evolution)

(Born: February 12, 1802, United Kingdom)
(Died: April 19, 1882, United Kingdom)

(His research was based on the collection of data during his sea voyage on HMS 'Beagle')

SCENE - 1

(On the stage is a table. Sitting before it, Darwin writes something and muses. Meanwhile enters Wallace)

Wallace : Well, Darwin, what are the plans?

Darwin : I will be a clergyman. I know my Holy Bible. Otherwise, the second choice: A doctor.

Wallace : You are my friend, Charles! I will not let you make a fool of yourself. Certainly, I am not more intelligent than you but definitely I am senior to you in age.

Darwin : What exactly are you trying to say?

Wallace : That is the trouble, if you do not find a reason, you try to find it.

Darwin : Come on. What are you trying to point out?

Wallace : All right. You are forcing me to answer. Suppose, you become a priest and by a slip, call 'Sun' the Moon, the Church will not pardon you. If as a doctor, you open the tummy of a patient to find a kidney infected and leave some instrument inside, you endanger the life of the patient. If the patient dies, your medical license will be cancelled. You can be punished also.

Darwin : Sounds like some mail-post has arrived.

Wallace : It is a ticket for a sea voyage.

Darwin : Let me see. It has been sent by a friend for a sea journey by HMS Beagle. See you after I return. I am off.

SCENE - 2

(On the stage, which looks like a ship, a mast is tied to a piece of wood. The captain of the ship, George Joseph, is there. A table is in the middle of the deck. Charles Darwin strolling on the deck and enjoying the heaving movement of the ship rolling on the waves.)

Darwin : Captain Joseph, can you please tell me where this glowing light house is?

Joseph : This is a British island and the glow indicates three deaths by hanging. This is an Indo-British colony, where a bloody revolution is about to take place.

(The captain moves onto the bow of the ship. Darwin is fully busy in writing something on the table. Wherever the ship docks, he is pleasantly surprised to

see the people, the birds, beasts and the trees there)

Darwin : Captain Joseph, don't you think it was quite an amazing sight in the Rann of the Backol Lake? Did you notice the beak of the birds? Beasts are the same but different somewhat from those of other islands? What do you say?

Joseph : It appears that by mistake your friend had told me that you were a scholar and a scientist.

Darwin : Why, any doubts?

Joseph : You are a crazy fellow. I have to take care of all the passengers and control the ship also. I cannot dance on your order all the time.

(Darwin is back home after a six month long sea voyage. Wallace and Darwin hug warmly.)

Darwin : This bag contains all my papers. Will you please keep it in my room? I am very tired.

Wallace : My dear friend, you have returned from such a long tour. Will you tell us anything about it?

Darwin : First, you tell me, what have you been doing?

Wallace : I have an invite for Australia.

Darwin : *(Sipping coffee)* If the proposal sounds good and suits you, please go, by all means. Perhaps you want to know what did I see? Honestly, my answer will be: What did I make out of it? I saw a lot of things about evolution of beings and I wrote them down on paper. All my impressions.

Wallace : Give some examples.

Darwin : Who were our ancestors? I mean, of us the humans. My answer: Monkey. The ape. But it must have taken thousands of years for this to happen.

Wallace : Fine, you had better take some rest. I have to attend to other things.

(Darwin returns to his room while Wallace addresses the people.)

It took me some two months to read and understand Darwin's Theory. Darwinian evolution means progressive development, development of the world and everything in it by a gradual process, in stages: For instance, the world is convinced that there were dinosaurs by looking at their fossils that have been found in many places. But the Nature, with its scheme of diversity and change, transformed the gigantic animals into smaller beasts. Darwin further writes that the world is engaged in a constant struggle -- "kill or be killed", also known by the theory of "survival of the fittest". Who lives and survives is the best.

I think Darwin is now ready to talk after having a rest. Now hear from his own mouth.

Darwin : Thank you Wallace dear! Nature fashions us in its own mould. I have measured the beaks of the birds. I have noticed their different sizes. Some birds feed on seeds, some live on honey from flowers. Every island has been cast by nature, according to its own design. Some beaks are designed for eating flesh, while some for pecking holes in trees. Now I have understood-whichever part of the anatomy is used more often is made bigger and stronger by Nature. See, the long neck of the giraffe. As long as fruits and leaves were easily available on the ground, it was all right but when they began to grow higher up in the trees, their neck became longer so that they could pluck leaves and fruits from a height of about 10-15 feet. Also, the volleyball players, who smash or service the ball over the net, have larger feet. All this is written in my book *The Voyage of the Beagle* (*The Origin of the Species*). To appreciate the strange things we see today, the theory of evolution is the best guide. Now I am going to cite an example with my friend here. *(Wallace mimics a monkey and produces similar sounds).*

Darwin : Hey Wallace! What is this? Come here. *(Wallace moves like a monkey and then straightens up like a man).*

Thank you Wallace. *(Embraces him. Wallace leaves the stage.)*

So, you see. Wallace was a monkey at that end but by the time he came near me, he became a human being. But it has taken millions of years to happen so.

This must be understood. Finally, I would like to say two things: Life in beings must have preceded lifeless matter like ammonia, phosphorus or light skimming over brackish water in a ravine or heat or lightening and now in the end -- let me state that I, Charles Darwin, belonging to the human species, is no believer in any Holy Book. Dear friend, now become a giraffe and eat leaves and fruits around you. *(The friends now imitate a giraffe, but his neck remains the same, like that of any normal human being.)*

Darwin : Well done. Now come to me. *(Wallace raises is right hand while with the other he seems to be eating leaves)* Thank you again, Wallace.

I am trying to demonstrate that when vegetation around the habitat of the giraffe becomes non-existent, it grows a longer neck to feed on leaves and fruits at a height. This process must have taken some half a million years. This is my Theory of Evolution.

CHAPTER - 39

The Last of the Subjects

(Royal Court of the Kingdom of Balpur where the king is held prisoner. Charges framed by Chetayya.)

King : All right, I will answer to the questions.

Chetayya : One accused of the conspiracy to kill the late king was your close friend?

King : Yes, it was my fault to show Swapnila the way to the palace. But the late king Mahan of Kajnapur was a characterless person. Swapnila was the result of one of his 'illicit affair'.

Chetayya : Is it not a fact that misled by that so-called astrologer, you stopped the digging of wells, water-bodies for the livestock and building of canals and waterways?

King : Yes, I do admit to this lapse on my part.

Chetayya : Harvested with the sweat of the people, you sold away granaries of foodgrains to other kingdoms on reduced price without the consent of your subjects. Was their approval not required?

King : I thought it was not necessary.

Chetayya : You started construction of the alloy memorial for the late king Mahan, when there were no funds left for the public welfare schemes in the royal treasury.

King : Stocks of alloys are the property of the king first.

Chetayya : All right. You are accused of suspending recruitment of soldiers, of strained relations with the neighbouring Kajnapur State, and because of failure to detect the evil designs of someone so close to you, you cannot be a person fit to be a king.

King : At the moment, this king surrounded by your bow-men is your prisoner.

Chetayya : You still believe that on the mineral wealth the first claim is that of the king and of the royalty, and not the subjects?

King : Yes, my answer is 'yes'.

Celaya : That crook Swapnila and her crooked astrology, which predicted turmoil in the sea and consequent rise in the sea-level, and you, without any thought or approval of the court, closed down all the projects. There was no turmoil in the sea. Instead, there was famine and hunger. You fool we have never before suffered such a huge loss of life and property. The people of Balpur were starved to death. And what did you do? You sold away food grain stocks to Kanjanapur on reduced rates.

King : Are you planning to cut me down in two parts?

Chetayya : Do not worry. The decision has not been taken yet. For your satisfaction, let me tell you that the blood and the smell of blood are the hallmarks of royal palaces. We know only to sow seeds in the fields and grow crops. Swapnila has brought this kingdom of Balpur to the brink of ruins. Just to avenge her hatred for her wicked progenitor (father), you went on throwing to the dogs, all the schemes of public good and the valuable minerals of the state. What you want is that we remain your humble servants for the whole life and keep worshiping you as if you are God. You want to exploit us. Isn't it?

King : Well, I am admitting my mistake.

Chetayya : Your acceptance is because of fear and not because of penitence. Before the people and the court, you, my king, are standing like a statue. It is therefore for me to come to a judgment.

(Chetayya takes a recess)

Gyanguru : We have to decide whether this former king and his advisors should be punished for knowingly or unknowingly abolishing schemes of public welfare and keeping the people in a state of want and poverty. Can a message go out from here to other rulers and countries that the good of people should be the top priority of all kings and government?

Chetayya : So, it seems you will not take a decision and instead want me to decide as to what should be done?

(Victory to Chetayya, long live Chetayya... slogans are raised)

A great sage has said that if there is a place full of controversy and the controversy is not resolved, it is better to leave that place for good. Therefore, we the subjects of this kingdom will leave this place and move away beyond its eastern and southern borders, where there is still a very large piece of land (territory) with plenty of water and vegetation untouched by human hand. Here, the people will be their own rulers. They will have their own fields and families, their domesticated animals and cattle as well as all their properties. What will not be there is a heartless king, like you, and his court and courtiers. Listen! Oh King, we are your last subjects.

(People on the stage leave, one by one, slowly)

King : Oh, no! Please listen. My dear Chaitayya do not leave me. Dear army chief, spiritual Gyanguru, stay on, please. I promise to set everything all right and restore all public welfare projects and schemes instantly.

CHAPTER - 40

Raghukul Reet

SCENE - 1 (YEAR 2000)

(Principal is sitting on the chair with table in front. Shantanu is standing. His father Sharmaji and Trivedi Sir are sitting on the other side.)

Principal : Speak Shantanu, what is the complaint?

Shantanu : Sir, Trivedi Sir has twisted my ears and also beaten me.

Principal : Is Shantanu telling the truth, Trivediji?

Trivedi Sir : Principal Sir, they create mischief in the class. I do speak sharply but never touch anyone. It is a lie that I have beaten anyone.

Shantanu : It is true. I can prove.

Principal : Do you have the proof of it?

Shantanu : Yes Sir, see here. He has been recorded beating me in the mobile.

Trivedi : Whose mobile is this?

Shantanu : This is Kalpana's mobile.

Trivedi : Right. Principal Sir, I will show you some of the videos of Shantanu and other boys and girls of the class.

Principal : Oh no! What is going on in the school?

Trivedi : Now that mobile days have come, these things will continue to happen.

Principal : If anyone brings the mobile to the school, I will seize it.

Trivedi : Do not do it, Sir, even by mistake. Students in another school have filed F.I.R. of theft with the police against the principal.

Principal : What do you say, Sharmaji?

Sharmaji : Well Sir, I had come today to say that you have not graced our dining table for a long time.

SCENE - 2 (YEAR 1950)

Principal : Yes, Trivediji. You have brought this naughty chap Shantanu with you. But why?

Trivedi Sir : The chowkidar says that he was trying to open the lock of the examination room.

Shantanu : Sir, you should think before accusing me. I am a national-level player. I needed the hockey. No room is marked as games room or examination room on a sign board. I was opening the lock of the room, which I thought was the games room.

Principal : Shantanu, games teacher Seth ma'am says that the key of the games room was with you.

Trivedi Sir : When you had the key of the games room, you should have opened that particular room. But how in God's name did you manage to open the examination room with it? Together, with being a national level player, you are also a 'Fraudia'.

Principal : Mind your language, Mr Trivedi. It is a fraud. That is the word. Where did you learn this, the other one?

Trivedi : In English, I have always called it "Fraudia". This is the language of our old Lucknow that I have known since boyhood.

Principal : Forget it, tell me, child, how did you open the lock of the examination room?

Shantanu : Sir, quite likely, Ma'am might have given to me by mistake the examination room key.

Principal : Catch your ears, bend and be a "Murga" right away. The examination room key always stays with me. It is right here, in the drawer of my table.

SCENE - 3 (YEARS 1900)

(Trivedi Sir is teaching tables to Shantanu)

Trivedi Sir : Six one is six.

Shantanu : Six one is six.

Trivedi Sir : Six twos are 12.

Shantanu : Six twos are 12.

Trivedi Sir : Six threes are eighteen.

Shantanu : Six twos are fourteen.

Trivedi Sir : Six threes are eighteen, Shantanu.

Shantanu : Six twos are sixteen.

Trivedi Sir : You fool six one is six, six twos are 12, six threes are 18.

Shantanu : Six one is six. Six twos are twelve. Six threes are thirteen.

Trivedi Sir : Now, if you don't repeat it correctly, you will be caned.

Shantanu : Six one is six. Six twos are twelve. Six threes are nineteen.

Trivedi Sir : Shantanu, go inside and get any thick cane that I use for dusting the carpet.

Shantanu : For what purpose will you use the cane, now?

Trivedi Sir : This cane is the table-learning machine. If your memory fails, it will refresh it instantly.

(Crying, while being caned)

Trivedi Sir : Now six one is six.

Shantanu : Six threes are eighteen.

Trivedi Sir : Six twos are twelve.

Shantanu : *Six fours are twenty four. Oh enough, Sir. (Takes away the cane and puts it aside and begins massaging the feet of Trivedi Sir.*

'Six eight are fourty eight...Now say six times nine fifty four. Ten times six are sixty... Oh No! Trivedi Sir is asleep.)

SCENE - 4 (YEAR 1850)

Guruji : Nattha, your son has not come today. Have you brought the fees or the gram flour? Arrears of fees are due. One full year has passed.

Nattha : Guruji, good news. Once again you have become a grandfather!

Guruji : Tell me Nattha. Shall I keep you, son, in Class VII or throw you out of the school?

Nattha : Now, cane me ten times, if you like. Neither do I have food grains nor fees to pay.

Guruji : It is all right with me.

(As Guruji gets up to pick the cane, Nattha begins running around the stage with Guruji in hot pursuit of him. Guruji tumbles and falls flat. Nattha rushes to pick Guruji and supports him to get back into the chair. Gives Guruji's body a massage.)

Nattha : Nothing to worry, Sir. A very minor dislocation of the collarbone. I have set it right by a light massage and manipulation of the right shoulder. Ask the lady at home to apply a little heated oil. You will be fine.

CHAPTER - 41

Bengali Doctor

SCENE 1

(80 miles away from the city is the village Sunderpur, wherethesonofaretiredarmymanhasreturnedhomeaftercompleting his medical education. The father-son duo enters the stage.)

Purushottam : (Talking to the spectators) My village folks, you know, the youngman standing by my side is my son. Ashutosh (who has returned home after obtaining his medical degree from Delhi), now you tell further.

Ashutosh : (Folds hands in greeting) I was born in this village. Had to work hard for my medical education. This is why I could not visit the village for years together.

Purushottam : Now, Dr Ashutosh will stay here at home and start a hospital in the village itself. Now, you my village brethren, will not have to rush to the city for normal operations and stitching of wounds.

(Amid shouts of Dr Ashutosh Zindabad and Purushottam Zindabad, rushes Khilawan on the stage. He is the childhood friend of Dr Ashutosh.)

Ashutosh : What is the matter, Khilawan? Looking

so troubled?

Khilawan : You are a qualified doctor. Pradhan *(village head)* Jiyalal of the nearby Kola village, perhaps you have heard of him, his son has been bitten by a snake.

Ashutosh : When?

Khilawan : About an hour ago or so.

Ashutosh : Has anyone seen the snake biting the boy? Is the snake-bite mark visible?

Khilawan : Oh, yes. The pradhan saw it himself. But the snake meanwhile crawled into a hole.

Ashutosh : Let me get my medical bag.

(Checks his injection kit. Let's go.)

SCENE - 2

(There is quite a crowd. A young boy is lying quietly on a charpoy. Khilawan introduces Dr Ashutosh to the Pradhan.)

Khilawan : This is Dr Ashutosh, who has done his MBBS from Delhi.

Pradhan : I have also sent for a doctor who should be here in a while. But please do whatever you can and save my son.

(Ashutosh examines the boy and covers his face with a sheet. Turns to Pradhan for a talk.)

Ashutosh : Pradhanji, I have checked the boy thoroughly with the stethoscope and the eye-torch. Felt the pulse also. There is no trace of life. Very sorry. I have arrived little late. The child is not alive any more.

Pradhanji : So, my son is no longer alive. You say

this upstart is a big doctor? *(Says with biting sarcasm).* Get lost. The Bengali doctor must be on his way. He brings back to life even those who have died of snake bite.

Khilawan : Doctor bhaiya, it is better to retreat. This is a village of notorious muscle men.

Ashutosh : But, I want to see how the Bengali doctor makes dead alive?

(Khilawan tried his best but fails to persuade Dr Ashutosh to return home. He merely moves on to stand under the shade of a tree. Meanwhile, the Bengali doctor enters the stage.)

Bengali Doctor : Pradhanji, why are you looking so sad?

Pradhanji : This young man is a city trained doctor. He is saying that my son is dead.

Bengali Doctor : But, I was told that it is a case of snake-bite? Anyway, dead or alive, I will see to it that he lives (remarks snidely). Such young men, who waste time on education, are a burden on their parents. My special diploma in snake-bite treatment is more special than paper degree. Now, show me where the snake bit the boy.

(Looking at the bite sign)

Pradhanji : Get some hot water from inside.

Bengali Doctor : Good that you already have hot water ready.

(Fills the ears and nostrils with water, when suddenly a thin plume of black smoke emanates from the nose and ears.)

Now, the job has been done. After an hour,

give the patient some warm milk to drink. Please pay my fees of Rs 100. I have to visit another village also to attend to a similar case of snake-bite. It is a girl, this time. You see, this is rainy season when snakes often come out of their holes.

Pradhanji : You came here in the nick of time, doctor sab! Here is your fee of 100 rupees.

Ashutosh : Mr Bengali doctor. Wait a bit. You just cannot go away like this. You must stay for an hour or else I will call the police.

Bengali Doctor : What? Look at this young doctor. He is advising me? Pradhanji, did you notice what he said? Should I stay as he is ordering?

Pradhanji : I swear by my pradhan-ship. I find this young chap talking a lot of sense. Mr Bengali doctor, what is the harm in waiting for an hour? Any problem?

Bengali Doctor : Now, I cannot wait. I am sorry. I just cannot.

Pradhanji : Catch him. He should not be allowed to go away. (Keeping a watchful eye on the Bengali Doctor. They all wait for one full hour but the boy does not open his eyes.)

Pradhan : *(Tells his people)* Take out your 'lathies'. All of you. This Bengali takes us to be fools. *(Lathis appear on the stage)*

Dr Ashutosh : Pradhanji, please don't commit a second mistake. You have made one already. The one whom God has taken away cannot be brought back. Not by anyone, leave alone this wretched Bengali doctor. Such quacks have their use in bandaging small wounds, etc. only but he is a deceitful fellow.

Pradhan : You are Purushottamji's son. What a lucky father to have a son like you? If you stay on in the village, you will bring dimwits like me on the right track.

CHAPTER - 42

Chanakya

Birth: 376 B.C.-283 B.C., Taxila, Pakistan
Death: Patliputra, India
Book : *Arthshashtra*
Father: Chanak
Contribution: Author of *Arthshashtra*
Other names : Kautilya, Vishnu Gupta
Knowledge, wisdom: diplomacy, spying and intelligence, statecraft, public welfare, Akhand Bharat etc. accounting for his name Kautilya.

SCENE - 1

(On the stage, Raja Ghananand of the Nand Dynasty, Soldiers, Acharyas, Guests, Prasad distribution after "Puja")

Raja Ghananand : On this auspicious occasion, I request all of you to please come forward and accept the Prasad and the gifts. After two Brahmins, Chanakya steps forward with folded hands before the king.

Chanakya : Your Majesty, I, Acharya Chanakya, has humbly come to you to beg for a favour.

Ghananand : Yes, Acharya, what is that?

Chanakya : Maharaj, I am talking of an undivided and unified India *(Akhand Bharat)*. I request you to please exile that Greek Chieftain Selucus from the Puru state.

Ghananand : How dare you insult my guest in my own court? Selucus will be given total security as long as I am live.

Chanakya : I know, you had the king of Puru killed by Selucus.

Ghananand : Soldiers, throw this vermin out of the court!

Chanakya : *(In fury, loose the knot of his hair on head and lets it fall on his shoulders)* Hereby, I vow not to tie this knot ever again, until I have destroyed this Nand Dynasty totally.

(Leaves the stage in rage)

SCENE - 2

(Prince Chandragupta protects the modesty of an Indian maiden and kills the offending soldier, which is seen by Chanakya)

Chanakya : Prince Chandragupta, I have seen your bravery, patience, courage and respect for women.

Chandragupta : I think, if I am not mistaken, I am talking to the great Acharya Chanakya of Taxila *(Both embrace each other)*

Chanakya : I find that you possess all the qualities to be the king of Magadh, I mean you have all the virtues required for being an Emperor, the King of Kings. Why wait? Can we not invade Magadh with the forces of Parvartak?

(Battlefield -- Chanakya, Chandragupta and Parvartak together defeat and kill

the entire Nand dynasty. Chankaya ties the knot of his loose hair.)

SCENE - 3

Chandragupta : If today I am the king of Magadh, then you Acharya Kautilya, are the founder and protector of the Mauryan Empire with your far-sighted politics.

Chanakya : Chandragupta, my king. I am pained at the defeat of smaller kings on account of Alexander's invasion.

Chandragupta : Is Acharya foreseeing a political role for himself?

Chanakya : I wish to see India undivided and united as a huge and magnificent empire.

SCENE - 4

Chanakya : My dear pupil, I regard the state to be the result of pragmatic compromises that people make with each other. There is no "divine will" behind the establishment of the state.

Chandragupta : Yes, master, you mean the king…

Chanakya : Sure!

1. The (king) is like the human head. One of its own kind: Intelligent, courageous, persevering, disciplined, far-sighted and expert in warfare.

2. Amatya – Prime Minister, ministers, secretary and fearless administrative personnel.

3. Territory *(Land, people or population)*

get going and bring two bottles of orange-flavoured drink. Some roasted meat and a bit of namkin will do.

Madhav : The vendor wants money in advance. No credit!

Ghisu : Here is the money. *(Takes out from the pocket)* Throw it on his wretched face.

Madhav : But, Bapu, what will happen to Budhia's corpse?

Ghisu : First, bring the orange flavour!

(Both drink)

Ghisu : Don't be afraid. By day light, Budhia's dead body would have badly swollen, emitting foul smell, so foul that the villagers themselves would be compelled to wrap the body in a shroud and dispose it.

CHAPTER - 47

The Judge King

(The judge king is seated on the throne in the royal court. The Gyanguru is on the chair. The doorman calls.)

Doorman : Sohan versus Mohan, be present.

(Both enter the stage and bow to the king)

Raja : What is the case?

Guru : Your Majesty, the case is that Sohan and Mohan are step brothers. Sohan's thinking is ordinary and his intelligence is limited. Mohan, who is the elder one, is always on the lookout for chances to embarrass Sohan.

Raja : Gyanguru, what is the complaint now?

Gyanguru : Last year too, Mohan and Sohan had quarrelled but the soldiers had brought peace. Now, let Mohan and Sohan themselves state the nature of the current controversy.

Mohan : Raja Saheb, this happened some time ago. Sohan, who is my step brother, was plucking vegetables in the fields. I casually asked him about the possibility of rains in the first week of July.

Sohan : It must rain because it has rained always in July for the last so many years.

Mohan : You mean it must, therefore, rain in the first week of July.

Sohan : My dear elder brother, this is what precisely I am saying.

Mohan : All right, what if it does not rain?

Sohan : Brother Mohan, I am your younger brother and you are wiser also. But it is going to be true. It will rain in the first week of July. No doubt about it!

Mohan : I asked Sohan to put a bet on it.

Sohan : I replied in the affirmative, saying yes.

Mohan : Assuming it does not rain, what will then happen?

Sohan : Mohan Bhaiya, in that case you may lash me 50 times, and if you like, in the royal court itself.

Gyanguru : O king, in the month of June, temperature was very warm and this cunning Mohan had anticipated the result. It did not rain in the first week of July, and now having won the bet, he wants to whip his step brother Sohan in the court.

Raja : I have heard the problem from both of you – the complainant and the defence. Sohan, are you ready for the lashes?

Sohan : Yes, my judge king. I am ready to suffer lashes from Mohan Bhaiya but you are known all over the kingdom for doing justice and saving your subjects. You alone can save me.

Raja : All right, Mohan, you have won the bet and you can strike 50 lashes to Sohan but it should cause him no pain because your bet is about lashing only.

(Sohan shouts aloud with joy – Blessed be our judge king!)

CHAPTER - 48

Julius Caesar

(Playwright William Shakespeare)

SCENE - 1

(Residence of Julius Caesar)

Brutus : My dear citizens of Rome, you must be wondering to see me at the residence of Julius Caesar. The reason for keeping it a secret from you is that the Roman Senate has decided to crown Julius Caesar today.

(In the other part of the building, Brutus and Julius Caesar meet)

Brutus : Julius, are you ready to go? Are you?

Julius Caesar : No, I have no intention of going.

Brutus : Is the fatigue of the battle still there or is it some other reason?

Caesar : No. It is somewhat different. My wife has seen in a dream that I have been turned into a statue with holes through which blood is oozing. Tell the Senate, I am not coming today.

Brutus : Do not misinterpret the dream. It is in favour of the people of Rome. You are doing them a favour. The Senate wants to crown you today, but afterwards may crown someone else if you do not go.

Caesar : Oh yes, quite likely. I wonder why I did not think of it. Come on, let us go.

(Both step out. On the way, all conspirators get together. After hugging them, Julius Caesar is quite happy. Cassius retraces his steps and strikes the first blow with his sword at Caesar. The rest of them follow, hear and attack one by one. On a sign from Brutus, a senator takes Antony away to the other side of the stage. In the end, Brutus also thrusts the dagger in the heart of Julius Caesar.)

Caesar : Oh my! Brutus you too? Now I had better die.

(Caesar's corpse is lying on the ground when Antony returns)

Antony : Now, I know, these people have conspired together to murder Julius Caesar.

(Seeing the blood-spattered sword that killed Caesar, he says to the killers to murder him also)

Brutus : No. We won't kill you. You are misunderstanding us. Once you get to know the cause behind this murder, you will also join us.

Antony : At the time of the burial of Julius, I will deliver a speech.

Brutus : But I have a condition. The first speech should be mine in which I will explain to the people that the muder of Caesar has been for the good of Rome and the Romans. And in your speech, you will honour me. Do not speak against us, even by mistake.

Scene - 2

(The coffin of Julius Caesar is resting on the ground)

Brutus : I loved Julius more than you all. But even more than that, I love my country, Rome. Would you have liked to live as slaves of Julius or rather live as free citizens and see a free Rome after killing Caesar? I am also sorry at the killing of Julius but he had to be killed because of his soaring ambitions. I love both -- Romans and my Rome. This was the reason why Julius Caesar was killed.

(The people applaud 'Marcus Brutus' and shout slogans in his praise. Brutus departs as Antony enters the stage.)

Antony : My fellow Romans, my brothers, Julius had fought and won many wars for and on behalf of Rome. He brought uncountable wealth from conquered states and distributed it among the Roman citizens. If Julius were ambitious, would he have behaved like this? When, the poor wept, Caesar also wept. I offered the crown three times to Caesar on the prompting of the Senate. Every time he turned it down. He said that he was a soldier, what would he do with the crown?

(Takes out a paper from his pocket)

This is the will of Julius Caesar: Every Roman should be given 75 coins of silver and his gardens should be made the property of Roman citizens.

(The people shout praises of Julius Caesar and gazes with contempt at Brutus, who sensing violence from people, commits suicide with his own sword.)

CHAPTER - 49

Ab Tak (Rajak Sharma Show — Fictional)

(Now, about to begin is the country's most celebrated case with Rajak Sharma)

Rajak Sharma : You will see something new in today's Adalat. This Adalat is fictional where I am going to call Mahatma Gandhi, Father of the Nation, in the witness box.

(Gandhiji takes his seat)

The judge for today's show is freedom fighter, Honourable Gopal Krishna Gokhale. Before we ask Gandhiji questions, I would like to seek his blessings.

(Rajak Sharma bows to Gandhiji)

To prosecute Mahatma Gandhi, I ask your permission, Honourable Judge Gopal Krishna Gokhale.

(Gokhale strikes the gavel on the table)

Gokhale : Permission granted.

Rajak Sharma : Bapu, it is said, that for quite some time you have not been seen in Heaven. Where have you been these days?

Mahatma Gandhi : I had gone on a visit to hell!

Rajak : Any special reason?

Gandhiji : Actually, some of my colleagues were dispatched to hell, by mistake. I had gone to plead their case. Now they have been sent back to Heaven.

Rajak : Bapu, can you tell their names?

Gandhiji : I cannot recall their names at the moment. But if you come to Heaven, I will arrange a meeting of them with you.

Rajak : All right. I leave this matter for now. Here is another question. There was one Santoben who had come to you with her young son. She had told you about his excessive gur eating habit, which was not good. You had asked her to come after three months. Why?

Gandhiji : Ok, yes, I can remember. Santoben had come to Sabarmati Ashram at mid-day with her son. I had called her again six months later.

Rajak : What happened later?

Gandhiji : I told her son not to eat too much gur as it is not a good habit. His mother was right.

Rajak : But to tell her only this much, why did you call her to come after six months. You could have said the same then and there.

Gandhiji : The matter was that I myself was a gur addict, so, first, I had to improve my own self and get rid of this habit in 3 months. This explains why I had told her to come 3 months later.

Rajak : About Dalits, it is said that you failed to

bring B.R. Ambedkar to your point of view. What were the objections?

Gandhiji : I have never considered Dalits and Ambedkar different from myself. The Poona Pact between Ambedkar and me in Yervada Jail did not have Ambedkar's sincere consent—not from heart. Pressure was put on him. Conditions in the country were not good. It was with tears in his eyes, Ambedkar put his signature. As far I am concerned, I had even campaigned for cleaning of toilets in the plague-affected Dalit colonies. Ambedkar might have or might not have been in my favour then, but today Ambedkar and I are room partners.

(Questions from people)

Man No.1 : Bapu, seeing you today in person, I am both pleased and shedding tears of joy. Please say what must we the youth do?

Gandhiji : Power was with the English then, now it is with the Khadi-clad gentry. I will only say one thing and it is that our Constitution is the best. Chanakya had also said the same in his *Arthashastra* to some of the leaders of his times. *(Clapping)*

Man No. 2 : Bapu, in you estimation, which religion owns India?

Gandhiji : Look, there was a merger of some 546 big and small princely states with India after independence. The Constitution was also framed under Ambedkar's chairmanship. Now, the country will be governed in accordance with the Constitution. The people, their religion and their languages all are inclusive in India.

Rajak : You are accused of favouring Nehru too much?

Gandhiji : I must say that in our group of lawyers he was the youngest, very able and also a fighter. **But Congressmen did not agree that with independence achieved. The objective of Congress had been fulfilled and it should have been dismantled. (??????????)**

Rajak : Bapu, I hear that you were so angry that you were absent from that magnificent function when on August 15, 1947, the Union Jack was covered and the tricolour was hoisted from the ramparts of the Red Fort.

Gandhiji : Looks like, Rajak Sharma, you don't read history. I was on a hunger strike to stop communal killings in Noakhali in Bengal. It was only then that the people there put down their arms and Nehruji had intervened to end my fast. Remember, Mountbatten had then called me a one-man army! *(Clapping)*

Rajak : We hear that you had a soft corner for the English?

Gandhiji : This charge is absolutely correct. In fact, I had several of them as my friends. They had come from London and only adhered to the Law of England. My fight was against their unjust actions and greed. Personally, I never hated any one of them.

Rajak : You are accused of not saving Bhagat

Singh from being sent to the gallows?

Gandhiji : I have spent all my life fighting against violence and lived by non-violence. Come to think of it, I was in Yarvada Jail when Bhagat Singh was hanged. I had never tried to save myself. I hold that if a crime is committed one should be ready to suffer the penalty. Remember that Chauri-Chaura affair after which I had withdrawn my Non-cooperation Movement. Moreover, the pact was to be signed with Irwin and 90,000 revolutionaries were left off from jail. But I had to agree to one of their conditions that prisoners accused of violence will not be released.

Rajak : Gandhiji, this is the last charge on you that relations between you, Nehruji and Subhash Chandra Bose were not cordial because of hanging of Bhagat Singh and the defeat of your candidate for the Congress president post in the 1939 party elections.

Gandhiji : I have already referred to Bhagat Singh in connection with the previous charge on me. As about elections, one party wins and the other party loses. The Azad Hind Fauj wanted to counter violence with violence. I do not subscribe to this view even now. As to my differences with Bose in his broadcast over Radio Ceylone, Subhash Chandra Bose expressed his regard for me and had even appealed me for my support.

CHAPTER - 50

President A.P.J. Abdul Kalam (Missile Man)

Birth: October 15, 1931, Rameshwaram
Death: July 27, 2015, Shillong

SCENE - 1

(A school in Rameshwaram. On the stage – the Principal and two teachers are sitting. The third teacher is speaking.)

Teacher : Honourable Principal, colleagues and my dear children. About three months ago, I saw a pupil of mine go out of the class while the period was not yet over. Perhaps, he was trying to enter another classroom. I stopped him mid-way and struck him hard four times with my cane for his indiscipline. After that the boy went back to his class. I had not behaved like this for the first time but I did not know that only after a short time, the same pupil will pay me back almost with compound interest. I wish to call A.P.J. Abdul Kalam to the stage.

(Abdul Kalam gets up and goes to the teacher)

All of you must be wondering, what it is all this about? Well, I teach mathematics and just see how this boy responds to my four cane strikes! He scores 100 marks out of 100. Now, remember my prediction. I mean all of you here! This boy is going to grow up into a really great man, who will glorify the name of Rameshwaram in the country and the world. *(Loud Clapping)*

SCENE - 2

(Kalam is extremely busy with the SLV III – Launch Team, at the ISRO Headquarters. Enters the great scientist, Sarabhai. Both shake hands.)

Sarabhai : Did you notice, Kalam, when Prime Minister Indira Gandhi had talked about SLV III to ISRO, she perhaps had you in mind and that is how you were sent here as Project Director.

Kalam : Sir, the countdown has begun – 9, 8, 7, 6, 5, 4, 3, 2, 1 "Go". India's first SLV III has been launched. *(Both hug)*

Sarabhai : You have become the first all-conquering scientist of India.

Kalam : Sir, it is because of your good wishes and your scientific analysis. My entire SLV III Team and the country look upon you as an Ideal, the same way as I do.

Sarabhai : I have every hope that you will be able to place the Rohini Satellite in the orbit of the Earth like the way you had built a small helicopter for the Indian Army.

(Sarabhai leaves the stage, and Kalam is seen talking to the crowd)

Kalam : We are a nation which treads the path of 'Vasudhaiv Kutumbakam', that is 'the world is a family'. Our neighbouring country is however arming itself with the most modern weapons. Therefore, we also must give attention to our own security and ability to strike in defense. The cost of the three missiles that is Agni, Prithvi and Trishul, together with ancillaries to blast them off, runs into crores of rupees.

SCENE - 3

(After retirement from ISRO, A.P.J. takes up a teaching job in a university in Chennai. One day while he was lecturing the class, there came an urgent call from the government at the center. Prime Minister Atal Bihari Vajpayee told Kalam that his party wants to nominate him for the nation's highest office, The President of India)

Kalam : You have already decorated me with Bharat Ratna, the highest national honour. Please spare me an hour and I will let you know.

(After some time, addressing students in a school)

Student 1 : How to deal with failure?

Kalam : First of all, we must try to find out the cause of it. Then we can overcome failure.

Student 2 : For doing something constructive, one must concentrate hard on an idea. What do you say, Sir?

Kalam : What you have asked is constructive in itself. Yes, you have to have an idea. Now to explain it further will require a lot of time and thinking.

Student 3 : How can the youth achieve success in life?

Kalam : You must have (1) A Noble Objective (2) The desire to expand the frontiers of your knowledge (3) Appetite for hard work (4) Persistence till perfection is achieved. (While still speaking Kalam Sahab suddenly falters and falls on the table in front)

(APJ Abdul Kalam is no more)

